My Complete Program New Cookbook 2024

Quick, Delicious, and Nutritious Recipes: Enjoy Healthy Freestyle Meals for Weight Loss and Improved Well-being

Dr Emmy Mack

CONTENTS

INTRODUCTION

Welcome to a delicious and nutritious journey! This cookbook will help you achieve a well-rounded and energetic lifestyle with the WW program. Having worked as a doctor for many years, I have witnessed the incredible impact that a healthy diet can have on one's well-being. My path to wellness had its fair share of bumps along the way. Similar to many others, I faced challenges in finding a sustainable approach to food that struck a balance between enjoyment and healthy choices. Everything fell into place for me when I found the program.

This book offers much more than a mere compilation of recipes. This is the result of my extensive experience and deep passion for assisting individuals in reaching their health objectives. Each recipe in this book has been carefully crafted and tested to prioritize both taste and health, helping you on your journey toward a healthier lifestyle.

I'll provide more than just recipes; I'll offer practical advice and guidance on mindful eating to help you cultivate a healthy relationship with food. I'll also share helpful tips for making wise decisions while cooking at home or eating out, so you can stay on track regardless of the circumstances.

To make healthy eating even healthier, I've included a variety of recipes with zero points. Alright, let's get started. Take a moment to relax, open up this book, and let's begin our journey together. With every delightful dish, you're not just preparing food—you're crafting a more nourishing and joyful version of yourself!

Welcome to the World of Flavorful, Healthy Cooking

Join me on a flavorful adventure as we explore the intersection of deliciousness and health in this cookbook. Whether you're an experienced cook or new to the kitchen, these recipes are here to satisfy your taste buds while helping you achieve your health goals. Our menu features a wide range of delicious options, from refreshing salads to comforting stews. Every dish has been carefully prepared to perfectly balance flavor, nutrition, and satisfaction.

What to Expect

- **Delicious Ingredients**: Our recipes feature fresh produce, lean proteins, and whole grains. Wholesome ingredients are the foundation of great meals.

- **Smart Points System**: Each recipe in the cookbook is accompanied by its corresponding Smart Points values. These values are designed to assist you in making informed decisions and staying on course with your weight loss or maintenance journey.

- **Cooking Tips and Techniques**: I will provide helpful kitchen tips, tricks, and techniques to improve your culinary skills. I have you covered when it comes to mastering a perfect stir-fry or baking a guilt-free dessert.

- **Community and Support**: Become a part of our community of food enthusiasts who love to share their experiences, adaptations, and success stories. It's much more enjoyable to cook when we work as a team!

Let's get ready to cook! Put on your apron, sharpen your knives, and prepare to make delicious meals that will nourish your body and soul. Enjoy your time in the kitchen!

Explore the rest of the cookbook, and may your kitchen be filled with happiness and delicious meals!

Chapter 1: Breakfast

Blueberry Almond Overnight Oats

Time to Prepare: 10 minutes
Cooking Time: 0 minutes
Number of Servings: 1

Ingredients:

- 1/2 cup of rolled oats
- 1/2 cup of unsweetened almond milk
- 1/4 cup of Greek yogurt (non-fat)
- 1/2 cup of fresh blueberries
- 1 tablespoon sliced almonds
- 1 teaspoon of chia seeds
- 1/2 teaspoon of vanilla extract
- 1 teaspoon of honey (optional)

Instructions List:

1. In a mason jar or bowl, combine rolled oats, almond milk, Greek yogurt, chia seeds, and vanilla extract. Stir well to combine.
2. Gently fold in the fresh blueberries.
3. Cover and refrigerate overnight or for at least 4 hours.
4. Before serving, stir the oats and top with sliced almonds.
5. Drizzle with honey if desired.

Nutritional Information (per serving):

- Calories: 280
- Protein: 10g
- Total Fats: 7g
- Fiber: 7g
- Carbohydrates: 44g

Points: 5 Points

Veggie-Packed Breakfast Burrito

Time to Prepare: 10 minutes
Cooking Time: 10 minutes
Number of Servings: 1

Ingredients:

- 1 whole wheat tortilla

- 1/2 cup of egg whites
- 1/4 cup of black beans, rinsed and drained
- 1/4 cup of diced bell peppers
- 1/4 cup of diced tomatoes
- 1/4 cup of spinach, chopped
- 1/4 avocado, sliced
- 2 tablespoons salsa
- Salt and pepper to taste
- Cooking spray

Instructions List:

1. Spray a non-stick skillet with cooking spray and heat over medium heat.
2. Add bell peppers and tomatoes to the skillet, cooking for 2-3 minutes until they start to soften.
3. Add spinach and cook for another minute until wilted.
4. Pour in the egg whites and cook, stirring occasionally, until scrambled and fully cooked.
5. Warm the tortilla in the microwave for 10-15 seconds.
6. Place the egg white mixture, black beans, and avocado slices in the center of the tortilla.
7. Top with salsa, then roll up the tortilla, folding in the sides to form a burrito.
8. Serve immediately.

Nutritional Information (per serving):

- Calories: 300
- Protein: 20g
- Total Fats: 10g
- Fiber: 10g
- Carbohydrates: 35g

Points: 6 Points

Banana Pancakes

Time to Prepare: 5 minutes
Cooking Time: 10 minutes
Number of Servings: 1

Ingredients:

- 1 ripe banana
- 2 eggs
- 1/2 teaspoon of baking powder

- 1/2 teaspoon of vanilla extract
- Cooking spray

Instructions List:

1. In a bowl, mash the ripe banana until smooth.
2. Add the eggs, baking powder, and vanilla extract to the mashed banana, and mix until well mixed.
3. Spray a non-stick skillet with cooking spray and heat over medium heat.
4. Pour small amounts of the batter into the skillet to form pancakes.
5. Cook for 2-3 minutes on each side, or until golden brown.
6. Serve immediately.

Nutritional Information (per serving):

- Calories: 210
- Protein: 12g
- Total Fats: 7g
- Fiber: 3g
- Carbohydrates: 30g

Points: 0 Points

Egg Muffins

Time to Prepare: 10 minutes
Cooking Time: 20 minutes
Number of Servings: 6

Ingredients:

- 6 eggs
- 1/2 cup of diced bell peppers
- 1/2 cup of chopped spinach
- 1/4 cup of diced onion
- 1/4 cup of diced tomatoes
- Salt and pepper to taste
- Cooking spray

Instructions List:

1. Preheat the oven to 375°F (190°C).
2. Spray a muffin tin with cooking spray.
3. In a large bowl, whisk the eggs until well beaten.
4. Add the bell peppers, spinach, onion, and tomatoes to the eggs. Season with salt and pepper, and mix well.

5. Pour the egg mixture evenly into the muffin tin cups.

6. Bake for 20 minutes, or until the egg muffins are set and lightly golden.

7. Allow to cool slightly before serving.

Nutritional Information (per serving):

- Calories: 70

- Protein: 6g

- Total Fats: 4g

- Fiber: 1g

- Carbohydrates: 2g

Points: 0 Points

Tofu Scramble

Time to Prepare: 10 minutes
Cooking Time: 10 minutes
Number of Servings: 2

Ingredients:

- 1 block (14 oz) firm tofu, drained and crumbled

- 1/2 cup of diced bell peppers

- 1/2 cup of diced onions

- 1 cup of spinach, chopped

- 1 teaspoon of turmeric

- 1/2 teaspoon of garlic powder

- Salt and pepper to taste

- Cooking spray

Instructions List:

1. Spray a non-stick skillet with cooking spray and heat over medium heat.

2. Add the diced onions and bell peppers to the skillet, cooking until softened, about 3-4 minutes.

3. Add the crumbled tofu to the skillet and stir in the turmeric, garlic powder, salt, and pepper. Cook for 5-7 minutes, stirring occasionally.

4. Add the chopped spinach and cook for another 1-2 minutes, until wilted.

5. Serve hot.

Nutritional Information (per serving):

- Calories: 120

- Protein: 12g

- Total Fats: 7g

- Fiber: 3g

- Carbohydrates: 8g

Points: 0 Points

Greek Yogurt Parfait with Mixed Berries

Time to Prepare: 5 minutes
Cooking Time: 0 minutes
Number of Servings: 1

Ingredients:

- 1 cup of non-fat Greek yogurt

- 1/2 cup of mixed berries (strawberries, blueberries, raspberries)

- 1 tablespoon honey

- 2 tablespoons granola

Instructions List:

1. In a serving glass or bowl, layer half of the Greek yogurt.

2. Add half of the mixed berries on top of the yogurt.

3. Drizzle with half of the honey.

4. Repeat the layers with the remaining yogurt, berries, and honey.

5. Sprinkle the granola on top.

6. Serve immediately.

Nutritional Information (per serving):

- Calories: 200

- Protein: 14g

- Total Fats: 3g

- Fiber: 4g

- Carbohydrates: 32g

Points: 3 Points

Avocado Toast with Poached Egg

Time to Prepare: 5 minutes
Cooking Time: 5 minutes
Number of Servings: 1

Ingredients:

- 1 slice whole grain bread

- 1/2 avocado, mashed

- 1 egg
- 1 teaspoon of lemon juice
- Salt and pepper to taste
- Cooking spray

Instructions List:

1. Toast the slice of whole grain bread.

2. In a small bowl, mix the mashed avocado with lemon juice, salt, and pepper.

3. Spread the avocado mixture evenly on the toasted bread.

4. Spray a small saucepan with cooking spray and fill it with water. Bring the water to a simmer.

5. Crack the egg into a small bowl, then gently slide it into the simmering water. Poach for 3-4 minutes, until the white is set and the yolk is still runny.

6. Using a slotted spoon, remove the poached egg from the water and place it on top of the avocado toast.

7. Season with additional salt and pepper if desired. Serve immediately.

Nutritional Information (per serving):

- Calories: 250
- Protein: 10g
- Total Fats: 18g
- Fiber: 7g
- Carbohydrates: 20g

Points: 5 Points

Quinoa Breakfast Bowl

Time to Prepare: 10 minutes
Cooking Time: 15 minutes
Number of Servings: 1

Ingredients:

- 1/2 cup of cooked quinoa
- 1/4 cup of black beans, rinsed and drained
- 1/4 avocado, diced
- 1/4 cup of cherry tomatoes, halved
- 1/4 cup of spinach, chopped
- 1 egg
- 1 tablespoon salsa
- 1 teaspoon of olive oil

- Salt and pepper to taste

- Cooking spray

Instructions List:

1. Spray a non-stick skillet with cooking spray and heat over medium heat.

2. Add the spinach and cook until wilted, about 2 minutes.

3. In a bowl, combine the cooked quinoa, black beans, avocado, cherry tomatoes, and cooked spinach. Season with salt and pepper.

4. In the same skillet, add olive oil and cook the egg sunny side up or to your desired doneness.

5. Top the quinoa mixture with the cooked egg and salsa.

6. Serve immediately.

Nutritional Information (per serving):

- Calories: 320

- Protein: 13g

- Total Fats: 17g

- Fiber: 9g

- Carbohydrates: 34g

Points: 6 Points

Cottage Cheese Pancakes

Time to Prepare: 5 minutes
Cooking Time: 10 minutes
Number of Servings: 1

Ingredients:

- 1/2 cup of cottage cheese (low-fat)

- 1/4 cup of rolled oats

- 2 eggs

- 1/2 teaspoon of baking powder

- 1/2 teaspoon of vanilla extract

- Cooking spray

Instructions List:

1. In a blender, combine cottage cheese, rolled oats, eggs, baking powder, and vanilla extract. Blend until smooth.

2. Spray a non-stick skillet with cooking spray and heat over medium heat.

3. Pour small amounts of the batter into the skillet to form pancakes.

4. Cook for 2-3 minutes on each side, or until golden brown.

5. Serve immediately.

Nutritional Information (per serving):

- Calories: 240
- Protein: 22g
- Total Fats: 10g
- Fiber: 3g
- Carbohydrates: 16g

Points: 4 Points

Chapter 2: Appetizers and Snacks

Zucchini Fritters with Tzatziki

Time to Prepare: 15 minutes
Cooking Time: 10 minutes
Number of Servings: 4

Ingredients:

- 2 medium zucchinis, grated
- 1/2 cup of whole wheat breadcrumbs
- 2 eggs
- 2 cloves garlic, minced
- 2 tablespoons chopped fresh dill
- Salt and pepper to taste
- Cooking spray

Tzatziki:

- 1/2 cup of non-fat Greek yogurt
- 1/4 cup of grated cucumber
- 1 clove garlic, minced
- 1 tablespoon lemon juice
- 1 tablespoon chopped fresh dill
- Salt and pepper to taste

Instructions List:

1. Place the grated zucchini in a colander, sprinkle with salt, and let it sit for 10 minutes. Squeeze out excess moisture from the zucchini using paper towels.
2. In a large bowl, combine the grated zucchini, breadcrumbs, eggs, minced garlic, chopped dill, salt, and pepper. Mix well.
3. Heat a non-stick skillet over medium heat and spray with cooking spray.
4. Drop spoonfuls of the zucchini mixture onto the skillet, flattening them with a spatula. Cook for 3-4 minutes on each side, or until golden brown and cooked through.
5. Meanwhile, prepare the tzatziki by mixing together the Greek yogurt, grated cucumber, minced garlic, lemon juice, chopped dill, salt, and pepper in a bowl.
6. Serve the zucchini fritters hot with tzatziki on the side.

Nutritional Information (per serving):

- Calories: 150
- Protein: 10g
- Total Fats: 3g

- Fiber: 3g
- Carbohydrates: 20g

Points: 3 Points

Amazing Deviled Eggs

Time to Prepare: 15 minutes
Cooking Time: 10 minutes (for boiling eggs)
Number of Servings: 6

Ingredients:

- 6 large eggs
- 2 tablespoons non-fat Greek yogurt
- 1 teaspoon of Dijon mustard
- 1 teaspoon of white vinegar
- Salt and pepper to taste
- Paprika, for garnish
- Chopped fresh chives, for garnish

Instructions List:

1. Place the eggs in a pot and cover with cold water. Bring to a boil over high heat.
2. Once boiling, cover the pot and remove from heat. Let the eggs sit in the hot water for 10-12 minutes.
3. Drain the hot water and transfer the eggs to a bowl of ice water to cool completely.
4. Once cooled, peel the eggs and slice them in half lengthwise. Remove the yolks and place them in a separate bowl.
5. Mash the egg yolks with a fork until smooth. Add Greek yogurt, Dijon mustard, white vinegar, salt, and pepper. Mix until well mixed.
6. Spoon the yolk mixture back into the egg white halves.
7. Garnish with a sprinkle of paprika and chopped fresh chives.
8. Serve chilled.

Nutritional Information (per serving):

- Calories: 70
- Protein: 6g
- Total Fats: 4g
- Fiber: 0g
- Carbohydrates: 1g

Points: 0 Points

Buffalo Chicken Celery Bites

Time to Prepare: 10 minutes
Cooking Time: 0 minutes
Number of Servings: 4

Ingredients:

- 2 cups of cooked shredded chicken breast
- 1/4 cup of hot sauce (such as Frank's RedHot)
- 2 tablespoons non-fat Greek yogurt
- 2 tablespoons chopped celery
- 2 tablespoons chopped green onions
- Salt and pepper to taste
- 8 celery stalks, cut into bite-sized pieces

Instructions List:

1. In a mixing bowl, combine the shredded chicken, hot sauce, Greek yogurt, chopped celery, and chopped green onions. Mix well.
2. Season with salt and pepper to taste.
3. Spoon the buffalo chicken mixture onto the celery pieces, dividing evenly.
4. Serve immediately.

Nutritional Information (per serving):

- Calories: 120
- Protein: 20g
- Total Fats: 2g
- Fiber: 2g
- Carbohydrates: 4g

Points: 0 Points

Hummus

Time to Prepare: 10 minutes
Cooking Time: 0 minutes
Number of Servings: 8

Ingredients:

- 2 cans (15 ounces each) chickpeas, drained and rinsed
- 1/4 cup of tahini
- 1/4 cup of lemon juice
- 2 cloves garlic, minced

- 1/2 teaspoon of ground cumin
- Salt to taste
- 2 tablespoons water (optional, for desired consistency)
- Paprika and olive oil, for garnish

Instructions List:

1. In a food processor, combine the chickpeas, tahini, lemon juice, minced garlic, ground cumin, and salt.
2. Blend until smooth, scraping down the sides of the bowl as needed. If the hummus is too thick, add water, 1 tablespoon at a time, until desired consistency is reached.
3. Transfer the hummus to a serving bowl.
4. Drizzle with olive oil and sprinkle with paprika for garnish.
5. Serve with your favorite vegetables or whole grain crackers.

Nutritional Information (per serving):

- Calories: 110
- Protein: 5g
- Total Fats: 5g
- Fiber: 4g
- Carbohydrates: 14g

Points: 0 Points

Mini Turkey Meatballs

Time to Prepare: 15 minutes
Cooking Time: 15 minutes
Number of Servings: 4

Ingredients:

- 1 pound lean ground turkey
- 1/4 cup of breadcrumbs
- 1/4 cup of grated Parmesan cheese
- 1 egg
- 2 cloves garlic, minced
- 2 tablespoons chopped fresh parsley
- 1 teaspoon of dried oregano
- Salt and pepper to taste
- Cooking spray

Instructions List:

1. Preheat the oven to 400°F (200°C). Line a baking sheet with parchment paper and lightly coat with cooking spray.

2. In a large mixing bowl, combine the ground turkey, breadcrumbs, Parmesan cheese, egg, minced garlic, chopped parsley, dried oregano, salt, and pepper. Mix until well mixed.

3. Roll the mixture into small balls, about 1 inch in diameter, and place them on the prepared baking sheet.

4. Bake in the preheated oven for 12-15 minutes, or until the meatballs are cooked through and lightly browned on the outside.

5. Serve hot with your favorite dipping sauce or add to pasta dishes or salads.

Nutritional Information (per serving):

- Calories: 190

- Protein: 20g

- Total Fats: 8g

- Fiber: 1g

- Carbohydrates: 8g

Points: 3 Points

Cucumber Slices with Herbed Cream Cheese

Time to Prepare: 10 minutes
Cooking Time: 0 minutes
Number of Servings: 4

Ingredients:

- 1 large cucumber, sliced

- 1/2 cup of reduced-fat cream cheese, softened

- 1 tablespoon chopped fresh dill

- 1 tablespoon chopped fresh chives

- Salt and pepper to taste

Instructions List:

1. In a small bowl, mix together the softened cream cheese, chopped fresh dill, chopped fresh chives, salt, and pepper until well mixed.

2. Spread a thin layer of the herbed cream cheese onto each cucumber slice.

3. Arrange the cucumber slices on a serving platter.

4. Serve immediately, or refrigerate until ready to serve.

Nutritional Information (per serving):

- Calories: 60

- Protein: 2g

- Total Fats: 4g

- Fiber: 1g
- Carbohydrates: 5g

Points: 1 Point

Guacamole-Stuffed Cherry Tomatoes

Time to Prepare: 15 minutes
Cooking Time: 0 minutes
Number of Servings: 4

Ingredients:

- 16 cherry tomatoes
- 1 ripe avocado
- 1 tablespoon lime juice
- 1/4 teaspoon of garlic powder
- 1/4 teaspoon of onion powder
- Salt and pepper to taste
- 1 tablespoon chopped fresh cilantro (optional)
- Hot sauce (optional)

Instructions List:

1. Slice the tops off the cherry tomatoes and scoop out the seeds and pulp using a small spoon. Place the hollowed-out tomatoes upside down on a paper towel to drain excess liquid.

2. In a small bowl, mash the ripe avocado with lime juice, garlic powder, onion powder, salt, and pepper until smooth.

3. If desired, mix in chopped fresh cilantro and hot sauce to taste.

4. Spoon the guacamole mixture into the hollowed-out cherry tomatoes, filling each one.

5. Arrange the stuffed cherry tomatoes on a serving platter.

6. Serve immediately, or refrigerate until ready to serve.

Nutritional Information (per serving):

- Calories: 70
- Protein: 2g
- Total Fats: 6g
- Fiber: 3g
- Carbohydrates: 4g

Points: 2 Points

Baked Sweet Potato Fries

Time to Prepare: 10 minutes
Cooking Time: 25 minutes
Number of Servings: 4

Ingredients:

- 2 large sweet potatoes, peeled and cut into fries
- 1 tablespoon olive oil
- 1 teaspoon of paprika
- 1/2 teaspoon of garlic powder
- 1/2 teaspoon of onion powder
- Salt and pepper to taste
- Cooking spray

Instructions List:

1. Preheat the oven to 425°F (220°C). Line a baking sheet with parchment paper and lightly coat with cooking spray.
2. In a large bowl, toss the sweet potato fries with olive oil, paprika, garlic powder, onion powder, salt, and pepper until evenly coated.
3. Arrange the seasoned sweet potato fries in a single layer on the prepared baking sheet.
4. Bake in the preheated oven for 20-25 minutes, flipping halfway through, until the fries are golden brown and crispy.
5. Remove from the oven and serve hot.

Nutritional Information (per serving):

- Calories: 140
- Protein: 2g
- Total Fats: 3g
- Fiber: 3g
- Carbohydrates: 27g

Points: 4 Points

Greek Yogurt Ranch Dip

Time to Prepare: 5 minutes
Cooking Time: 0 minutes
Number of Servings: 8

Ingredients:

- 1 cup of non-fat Greek yogurt
- 1 tablespoon dried dill

- 1 tablespoon dried parsley
- 1 teaspoon of garlic powder
- 1 teaspoon of onion powder
- 1/2 teaspoon of dried chives
- 1/2 teaspoon of paprika
- Salt and pepper to taste

Instructions List:

1. In a mixing bowl, combine the Greek yogurt, dried dill, dried parsley, garlic powder, onion powder, dried chives, paprika, salt, and pepper.

2. Stir until all ingredients are well mixed and the herbs and spices are evenly distributed throughout the yogurt.

3. Adjust seasoning to taste, if necessary.

4. Transfer the dip to a serving bowl.

5. Serve immediately or refrigerate until ready to serve.

Nutritional Information (per serving):

- Calories: 20
- Protein: 3g
- Total Fats: 0g
- Fiber: 0g
- Carbohydrates: 2g

Points: 1 Point

Caprese Skewers with Balsamic Glaze

Time to Prepare: 15 minutes
Cooking Time: 0 minutes
Number of Servings: 4

Ingredients:

- 16 cherry tomatoes
- 16 small fresh mozzarella balls (bocconcini)
- 16 fresh basil leaves
- 2 tablespoons balsamic glaze
- Salt and pepper to taste
- 8 skewers

Instructions List:

1. Thread a cherry tomato, a mozzarella ball, and a basil leaf onto each skewer, repeating until all ingredients are used.

2. Arrange the skewers on a serving platter.

3. Drizzle balsamic glaze over the skewers.

4. Season with salt and pepper to taste.

5. Serve immediately, or refrigerate until ready to serve.

Nutritional Information (per serving):

- Calories: 120

- Protein: 6g

- Total Fats: 7g

- Fiber: 1g

- Carbohydrates: 8g

Points: 3 Points

Chapter 3: Breads and Baked Goods

Whole Wheat Banana Bread

Time to Prepare: 15 minutes
Cooking Time: 1 hour
Number of Servings: 12

Ingredients:

- 3 ripe bananas, mashed
- 1/2 cup of unsweetened applesauce
- 1/4 cup of honey or maple syrup
- 1/4 cup of non-fat Greek yogurt
- 2 eggs
- 1 teaspoon of vanilla extract
- 1 1/2 cups of whole wheat flour
- 1 teaspoon of baking soda
- 1/2 teaspoon of baking powder
- 1/2 teaspoon of cinnamon
- 1/4 teaspoon of salt
- Cooking spray

Instructions List:

1. Preheat the oven to 350°F (175°C). Grease a 9x5-inch loaf pan with cooking spray.

2. In a large mixing bowl, combine mashed bananas, applesauce, honey or maple syrup, Greek yogurt, eggs, and vanilla extract. Mix well.

3. In a separate bowl, whisk together whole wheat flour, baking soda, baking powder, cinnamon, and salt.

4. Gradually add the dry ingredients to the wet ingredients, stirring until just mixed. Do not overmix.

5. Pour the batter into the prepared loaf pan.

6. Bake in the preheated oven for 55-60 minutes, or until a toothpick inserted into the center comes out clean.

7. Allow the banana bread to cool in the pan for 10 minutes, then transfer it to a wire rack to cool completely before slicing.

Nutritional Information (per serving):

- Calories: 130
- Protein: 3g
- Total Fats: 1g
- Fiber: 2g
- Carbohydrates: 28g

Points: 4 Points

Rosemary Olive Oil Focaccia

Time to Prepare: 2 hours
Cooking Time: 25 minutes
Number of Servings: 12

Ingredients:

- 1 1/2 cups of warm water
- 2 1/4 teaspoons of active dry yeast
- 1 tablespoon honey
- 3 1/2 cups of all-purpose flour
- 1/4 cup of olive oil
- 1 teaspoon of salt
- 2 tablespoons chopped fresh rosemary
- Coarse sea salt, for sprinkling

Instructions List:

1. In a large mixing bowl, combine warm water, active dry yeast, and honey. Let it sit for 5-10 minutes until frothy.
2. Add all-purpose flour, olive oil, and salt to the yeast mixture. Stir until a dough forms.
3. Transfer the dough to a floured surface and knead for 5-7 minutes until smooth and elastic.
4. Place the dough in a lightly greased bowl, cover with a clean kitchen towel, and let it rise in a warm place for 1 hour, or until doubled in size.
5. Preheat the oven to 400°F (200°C). Grease a baking sheet with olive oil.
6. Punch down the risen dough and transfer it to the prepared baking sheet. Press the dough into a rectangle shape.
7. Use your fingers to make dimples all over the surface of the dough.
8. Drizzle olive oil over the dough and sprinkle with chopped fresh rosemary and coarse sea salt.
9. Bake in the preheated oven for 20-25 minutes, or until the focaccia is golden brown on top.
10. Allow the focaccia to cool slightly before slicing. Serve warm.

Nutritional Information (per serving):

- Calories: 190
- Protein: 4g
- Total Fats: 6g
- Fiber: 1g
- Carbohydrates: 30g

Points: 3 Points

Pumpkin Spice Muffins

Time to Prepare: 15 minutes
Cooking Time: 20 minutes
Number of Servings: 12

Ingredients:

- 1 3/4 cups all-purpose flour
- 1 teaspoon of baking soda
- 1/2 teaspoon of baking powder
- 1/2 teaspoon of salt
- 1 teaspoon of ground cinnamon
- 1/2 teaspoon of ground ginger
- 1/4 teaspoon of ground nutmeg
- 1/4 teaspoon of ground cloves
- 1 cup of pumpkin puree
- 1/2 cup of brown sugar
- 1/4 cup of unsweetened applesauce
- 1/4 cup of maple syrup
- 1/4 cup of non-fat Greek yogurt
- 2 tablespoons olive oil
- 2 eggs
- 1 teaspoon of vanilla extract

Instructions List:

1. Preheat the oven to 375°F (190°C). Line a muffin tin with paper liners or lightly grease with cooking spray.

2. In a large mixing bowl, whisk together all-purpose flour, baking soda, baking powder, salt, cinnamon, ginger, nutmeg, and cloves.

3. In another bowl, combine pumpkin puree, brown sugar, applesauce, maple syrup, Greek yogurt, olive oil, eggs, and vanilla extract. Mix until well mixed.

4. Gradually add the wet ingredients to the dry ingredients, stirring until just mixed. Do not overmix.

5. Divide the batter evenly among the muffin cups, filling each about 2/3 full.

6. Bake in the preheated oven for 18-20 minutes, or until a toothpick inserted into the center comes out clean.

7. Remove from the oven and let the muffins cool in the pan for 5 minutes before transferring them to a wire rack to cool completely.

Nutritional Information (per serving):

- Calories: 160

- Protein: 3g

- Total Fats: 3g

- Fiber: 1g

- Carbohydrates: 30g

Points: 5 Points

Quinoa Flatbread

Time to Prepare: 10 minutes
Cooking Time: 20 minutes
Number of Servings: 6

Ingredients:

- 1 cup of cooked quinoa

- 1/4 cup of almond flour

- 2 tablespoons ground flaxseed

- 1/2 teaspoon of baking powder

- 1/2 teaspoon of garlic powder

- 1/2 teaspoon of dried oregano

- 1/4 teaspoon of salt

- 2 eggs

- 1/4 cup of unsweetened almond milk

- Cooking spray

Instructions List:

1. Preheat the oven to 375°F (190°C). Line a baking sheet with parchment paper and lightly coat with cooking spray.

2. In a large mixing bowl, combine cooked quinoa, almond flour, ground flaxseed, baking powder, garlic powder, dried oregano, and salt.

3. In a separate bowl, whisk together eggs and almond milk until well mixed.

4. Pour the egg mixture into the quinoa mixture and stir until evenly mixed and a dough forms.

5. Transfer the dough to the prepared baking sheet and use a spatula to spread it into a thin, even layer.

6. Bake in the preheated oven for 15-20 minutes, or until the flatbread is golden brown and crispy around the edges.

7. Remove from the oven and let it cool slightly before slicing into squares or triangles.

8. Serve warm as desired.

Nutritional Information (per serving):

- Calories: 100
- Protein: 5g
- Total Fats: 4g
- Fiber: 2g
- Carbohydrates: 10g

Points: 2 Points

Cheddar and Chive Biscuits

Time to Prepare: 15 minutes
Cooking Time: 15 minutes
Number of Servings: 12

Ingredients:

- 2 cups of all-purpose flour
- 2 teaspoons of baking powder
- 1/2 teaspoon of baking soda
- 1/2 teaspoon of salt
- 1/4 cup of cold unsalted butter, cut into small cubes
- 1 cup of shredded sharp cheddar cheese
- 1/4 cup of chopped fresh chives
- 3/4 cup non-fat buttermilk
- Cooking spray

Instructions List:

1. Preheat the oven to 450°F (230°C). Line a baking sheet with parchment paper and lightly coat with cooking spray.
2. In a large mixing bowl, whisk together all-purpose flour, baking powder, baking soda, and salt.
3. Add cold cubed butter to the flour mixture and use a pastry cutter or fork to cut the butter into the flour until the mixture resembles coarse crumbs.
4. Stir in shredded cheddar cheese and chopped fresh chives until evenly distributed.
5. Gradually add non-fat buttermilk to the flour mixture, stirring until just mixed and a dough forms. Do not overmix.
6. Turn the dough out onto a floured surface and knead gently for a few seconds until it comes together.
7. Pat the dough into a 1-inch thick circle. Use a biscuit cutter or the rim of a glass to cut out biscuits.
8. Place the biscuits on the prepared baking sheet, leaving a little space between each biscuit.
9. Bake in the preheated oven for 12-15 minutes, or until the biscuits are golden brown on top.

10. Remove from the oven and let the biscuits cool slightly before serving.

Nutritional Information (per serving):

- Calories: 150

- Protein: 6g

- Total Fats: 6g

- Fiber: 1g

- Carbohydrates: 19g

Points: 3 Points

Almond Flour Zucchini Bread

Time to Prepare: 15 minutes
Cooking Time: 50 minutes
Number of Servings: 12

Ingredients:

- 2 cups of almond flour

- 1 teaspoon of baking powder

- 1/2 teaspoon of baking soda

- 1/2 teaspoon of salt

- 1 teaspoon of ground cinnamon

- 1/4 teaspoon of ground nutmeg

- 3 large eggs

- 1/4 cup of honey or maple syrup

- 1/4 cup of unsweetened applesauce

- 1 teaspoon of vanilla extract

- 1 1/2 cups of grated zucchini (about 1 medium zucchini)

- Cooking spray

Instructions List:

1. Preheat the oven to 350°F (175°C). Grease a 9x5-inch loaf pan with cooking spray.

2. In a large mixing bowl, whisk together almond flour, baking powder, baking soda, salt, cinnamon, and nutmeg.

3. In another bowl, beat eggs. Add honey or maple syrup, unsweetened applesauce, and vanilla extract. Mix until well mixed.

4. Gradually add the wet ingredients to the dry ingredients, stirring until just mixed.

5. Fold in grated zucchini until evenly distributed throughout the batter.

6. Pour the batter into the prepared loaf pan, spreading it evenly.

7. Bake in the preheated oven for 45-50 minutes, or until a toothpick inserted into the center comes out clean.

8. Allow the zucchini bread to cool in the pan for 10 minutes, then transfer it to a wire rack to cool completely before slicing.

Nutritional Information (per serving):

- Calories: 160

- Protein: 6g

- Total Fats: 11g

- Fiber: 3g

- Carbohydrates: 12g

Points: 4 Points

Oatmeal Raisin Cookies

Time to Prepare: 15 minutes
Cooking Time: 10 minutes
Number of Servings: 24

Ingredients:

- 1 cup of old-fashioned oats

- 3/4 cup whole wheat flour

- 1/2 teaspoon of baking soda

- 1/2 teaspoon of ground cinnamon

- 1/4 teaspoon of salt

- 1/4 cup of unsalted butter, softened

- 1/4 cup of unsweetened applesauce

- 1/2 cup of brown sugar

- 1/4 cup of granulated sugar

- 1 large egg

- 1 teaspoon of vanilla extract

- 1/2 cup of raisins

Instructions List:

1. Preheat the oven to 350°F (175°C). Line a baking sheet with parchment paper.

2. In a large mixing bowl, combine oats, whole wheat flour, baking soda, cinnamon, and salt.

3. In another bowl, cream together softened butter, applesauce, brown sugar, and granulated sugar until smooth.

4. Add egg and vanilla extract to the butter mixture, beating until well mixed.

5. Gradually add the dry ingredients to the wet ingredients, mixing until just mixed.

6. Fold in raisins until evenly distributed throughout the dough.

7. Drop tablespoonfuls of dough onto the prepared baking sheet, spacing them about 2 inches apart.

8. Flatten each cookie slightly with the back of a spoon or your fingers.

9. Bake in the preheated oven for 8-10 minutes, or until the edges are golden brown.

10. Allow the cookies to cool on the baking sheet for 5 minutes, then transfer them to a wire rack to cool completely.

Nutritional Information (per serving):

- Calories: 80
- Protein: 1g
- Total Fats: 2g
- Fiber: 1g
- Carbohydrates: 15g

Points: 3 Points

Cornbread Muffins

Time to Prepare: 15 minutes
Cooking Time: 20 minutes
Number of Servings: 12

Ingredients:

- 1 cup of cornmeal
- 1 cup of all-purpose flour
- 1/4 cup of granulated sugar
- 1 tablespoon baking powder
- 1/2 teaspoon of salt
- 1 cup of unsweetened almond milk
- 1/4 cup of unsweetened applesauce
- 2 tablespoons honey
- 2 tablespoons olive oil
- 2 large eggs

Instructions List:

1. Preheat the oven to 400°F (200°C). Line a muffin tin with paper liners or lightly grease with cooking spray.

2. In a large mixing bowl, whisk together cornmeal, all-purpose flour, sugar, baking powder, and salt.

3. In another bowl, whisk together almond milk, applesauce, honey, olive oil, and eggs until well mixed.

4. Gradually add the wet ingredients to the dry ingredients, stirring until just mixed. Do not overmix.

5. Divide the batter evenly among the muffin cups, filling each about 2/3 full.

6. Bake in the preheated oven for 15-20 minutes, or until the muffins are golden brown on top and a toothpick inserted into the center comes out clean.

7. Remove from the oven and let the muffins cool in the pan for 5 minutes before transferring them to a wire rack to cool completely.

Nutritional Information (per serving):

- Calories: 140
- Protein: 3g
- Total Fats: 4g
- Fiber: 1g
- Carbohydrates: 23g

Points: 4 Points

Garlic Knots

Time to Prepare: 15 minutes
Cooking Time: 12 minutes
Number of Servings: 12

Ingredients:

- 1 pound pizza dough
- 2 tablespoons olive oil
- 2 cloves garlic, minced
- 1 tablespoon chopped fresh parsley
- Salt, to taste

Instructions List:

1. Preheat the oven to 400°F (200°C). Line a baking sheet with parchment paper.

2. Divide the pizza dough into 12 equal pieces. Roll each piece into a rope about 6 inches long.

3. Tie each rope into a knot and place it on the prepared baking sheet.

4. In a small bowl, combine olive oil, minced garlic, chopped fresh parsley, and a pinch of salt.

5. Brush the garlic mixture over the knots, ensuring they are well coated.

6. Bake in the preheated oven for 10-12 minutes, or until the knots are golden brown and cooked through.

7. Remove from the oven and serve warm.

Nutritional Information (per serving):

- Calories: 120
- Protein: 3g

- Total Fats: 4g

- Fiber: 1g

- Carbohydrates: 18g

Points: 2 Points

Lemon Poppy Seed Scones

Time to Prepare: 15 minutes
Cooking Time: 15 minutes
Number of Servings: 8

Ingredients:

- 2 cups of all-purpose flour

- 1/4 cup of granulated sugar

- 1 tablespoon baking powder

- 1/4 teaspoon of salt

- Zest of 1 lemon

- 1 tablespoon poppy seeds

- 1/2 cup of unsalted butter, cold and cut into small cubes

- 1/2 cup of non-fat plain Greek yogurt

- 1/4 cup of unsweetened almond milk

- 1 large egg

- 1 teaspoon of vanilla extract

Instructions List:

1. Preheat the oven to 400°F (200°C). Line a baking sheet with parchment paper.

2. In a large mixing bowl, whisk together flour, sugar, baking powder, salt, lemon zest, and poppy seeds.

3. Add cold cubed butter to the flour mixture. Using a pastry cutter or fork, cut the butter into the flour until the mixture resembles coarse crumbs.

4. In a separate bowl, whisk together Greek yogurt, almond milk, egg, and vanilla extract until well mixed.

5. Pour the wet ingredients into the dry ingredients and stir until just mixed. Be careful not to overmix.

6. Transfer the dough to a lightly floured surface and shape it into a circle about 1 inch thick.

7. Cut the dough into 8 equal wedges and place them on the prepared baking sheet.

8. Bake in the preheated oven for 12-15 minutes, or until the scones are golden brown on top.

9. Remove from the oven and let the scones cool on the baking sheet for a few minutes before transferring them to a wire rack to cool completely.

Nutritional Information (per serving):

- Calories: 250

- Protein: 5g

- Total Fats: 12g

- Fiber: 1g
- Carbohydrates: 30g

Points: 4 Points

Chapter 4: Poultry

Lemon Herb Grilled Chicken

Time to Prepare: 10 minutes
Cooking Time: 12 minutes
Number of Servings: 4

Ingredients:

- 4 boneless, skinless chicken breasts
- 2 tablespoons olive oil
- Zest and juice of 1 lemon
- 2 cloves garlic, minced
- 1 tablespoon chopped fresh parsley
- 1 tablespoon chopped fresh thyme
- Salt and pepper, to taste

Instructions List:

1. In a small bowl, whisk together olive oil, lemon zest, lemon juice, minced garlic, chopped parsley, chopped thyme, salt, and pepper to make the marinade.

2. Place the chicken breasts in a shallow dish or resealable plastic bag. Pour the marinade over the chicken, making sure each piece is well coated. Marinate in the refrigerator for at least 30 minutes, or up to 4 hours.

3. Preheat the grill to medium-high heat. Remove the chicken from the marinade and discard any excess marinade.

4. Grill the chicken breasts for 5-6 minutes per side, or until they are cooked through and have reached an internal temperature of 165°F (75°C).

5. Remove the chicken from the grill and let it rest for a few minutes before serving.

Nutritional Information (per serving):

- Calories: 230
- Protein: 28g
- Total Fats: 11g
- Fiber: 1g
- Carbohydrates: 2g

Points: 3 Points

Moroccan Spiced Chicken Tagine

Time to Prepare: 15 minutes
Cooking Time: 40 minutes
Number of Servings: 4

Ingredients:

- 4 boneless, skinless chicken thighs
- 1 tablespoon olive oil
- 1 onion, finely chopped
- 2 cloves garlic, minced
- 1 teaspoon of ground cumin
- 1 teaspoon of ground coriander
- 1 teaspoon of ground cinnamon
- 1/2 teaspoon of ground ginger
- 1/4 teaspoon of ground turmeric
- 1/4 teaspoon of ground paprika
- 1/4 teaspoon of ground cloves
- 1/4 teaspoon of ground black pepper
- 1/4 teaspoon of salt
- 1 can (14 oz) diced tomatoes, undrained
- 1/2 cup of low-sodium chicken broth
- 1/4 cup of chopped fresh cilantro
- 1 lemon, sliced
- Cooked couscous, for serving

Instructions List:

1. Heat olive oil in a large skillet or tagine over medium heat. Add chopped onion and minced garlic, and cook until softened, about 5 minutes.

2. Add ground cumin, ground coriander, ground cinnamon, ground ginger, ground turmeric, ground paprika, ground cloves, black pepper, and salt to the skillet. Stir well to combine.

3. Add chicken thighs to the skillet and cook until browned on all sides, about 5 minutes.

4. Stir in diced tomatoes and chicken broth. Bring the mixture to a simmer, then reduce the heat to low. Cover and cook for 25-30 minutes, or until the chicken is cooked through and tender.

5. Remove the lid and stir in chopped cilantro. Cook for an additional 5 minutes, or until the sauce has thickened slightly.

6. Serve the Moroccan spiced chicken tagine hot, garnished with lemon slices, alongside cooked couscous.

Nutritional Information (per serving):

- Calories: 320
- Protein: 28g
- Total Fats: 12g
- Fiber: 3g

- Carbohydrates: 24g

Points: 5 Points

Teriyaki Turkey Burgers

Time to Prepare: 15 minutes
Cooking Time: 12 minutes
Number of Servings: 4

Ingredients:

- 1 lb ground turkey

- 1/4 cup of low-sodium soy sauce

- 2 tablespoons honey

- 2 cloves garlic, minced

- 1 teaspoon of grated fresh ginger

- 1/4 teaspoon of black pepper

- 4 whole wheat hamburger buns

- Lettuce, tomato slices, and onion slices for topping (optional)

Instructions List:

1. In a mixing bowl, combine ground turkey, low-sodium soy sauce, honey, minced garlic, grated fresh ginger, and black pepper. Mix until well mixed.

2. Divide the turkey mixture into 4 equal portions and shape them into burger patties.

3. Preheat grill or grill pan over medium heat. Cook the turkey burgers for about 6 minutes per side, or until cooked through and no longer pink in the center.

4. Toast the whole wheat hamburger buns on the grill for a minute or until lightly toasted.

5. Assemble the burgers by placing each turkey patty on a bun and adding desired toppings such as lettuce, tomato slices, and onion slices.

6. Serve hot and enjoy!

Nutritional Information (per serving):

- Calories: 280

- Protein: 28g

- Total Fats: 8g

- Fiber: 2g

- Carbohydrates: 26g

Points: 4 Points

Tuscan Chicken Skillet

Time to Prepare: 15 minutes
Cooking Time: 25 minutes
Number of Servings: 4

Ingredients:

- 4 boneless, skinless chicken breasts
- Salt and pepper, to taste
- 1 tablespoon olive oil
- 2 cloves garlic, minced
- 1 onion, sliced
- 1 red bell pepper, sliced
- 1 yellow bell pepper, sliced
- 1 teaspoon of dried oregano
- 1 teaspoon of dried basil
- 1/2 teaspoon of dried thyme
- 1/4 teaspoon of red pepper flakes (optional)
- 1 can (14 oz) diced tomatoes, drained
- 1/2 cup of low-sodium chicken broth
- 2 cups of fresh spinach leaves
- 1/4 cup of grated Parmesan cheese

Instructions List:

1. Season chicken breasts with salt and pepper on both sides.

2. Heat olive oil in a large skillet over medium-high heat. Add chicken breasts and cook until browned on both sides and no longer pink in the center, about 6-8 minutes per side. Remove chicken from skillet and set aside.

3. In the same skillet, add minced garlic, sliced onion, and sliced bell peppers. Cook until vegetables are softened, about 5 minutes.

4. Stir in dried oregano, dried basil, dried thyme, and red pepper flakes (if using), and cook for another minute.

5. Add diced tomatoes and chicken broth to the skillet. Bring to a simmer.

6. Return chicken breasts to the skillet and nestle them into the sauce. Cook for 5 minutes, allowing flavors to meld.

7. Stir in fresh spinach leaves and cook until wilted.

8. Sprinkle grated Parmesan cheese over the top.

9. Serve hot and enjoy!

Nutritional Information (per serving):

- Calories: 280

- Protein: 34g

- Total Fats: 9g

- Fiber: 3g

- Carbohydrates: 14g

Points: 6 Points

Southern-Style Oven-Fried Chicken

Time to Prepare: 15 minutes
Cooking Time: 30 minutes
Number of Servings: 4

Ingredients:

- 4 boneless, skinless chicken breasts

- 1 cup of plain non-fat Greek yogurt

- 1 tablespoon Dijon mustard

- 1 teaspoon of paprika

- 1 teaspoon of garlic powder

- 1 teaspoon of onion powder

- 1/2 teaspoon of salt

- 1/4 teaspoon of black pepper

- 1 cup of whole wheat breadcrumbs

- Cooking spray

Instructions List:

1. Preheat the oven to 400°F (200°C). Line a baking sheet with parchment paper and set aside.

2. In a shallow dish, mix together Greek yogurt, Dijon mustard, paprika, garlic powder, onion powder, salt, and black pepper.

3. Place whole wheat breadcrumbs in another shallow dish.

4. Dip each chicken breast into the yogurt mixture, coating both sides evenly.

5. Then, dredge the chicken in the breadcrumbs, pressing gently to adhere.

6. Place the coated chicken breasts on the prepared baking sheet.

7. Lightly spray the top of each chicken breast with cooking spray.

8. Bake in the preheated oven for 25-30 minutes, or until the chicken is cooked through and golden brown.

9. Serve hot and enjoy!

Nutritional Information (per serving):

- Calories: 220

- Protein: 34g

- Total Fats: 2g

- Fiber: 1g

- Carbohydrates: 15g

Points: 0 Points

Buffalo Chicken Skewers with Blue Cheese Dipping Sauce

Time to Prepare: 15 minutes
Cooking Time: 15 minutes
Number of Servings: 4

Ingredients:

- 1 lb boneless, skinless chicken breasts, cut into cubes

- 1/4 cup of hot sauce

- 1 tablespoon olive oil

- 1 tablespoon honey

- 1 teaspoon of garlic powder

- 1/2 teaspoon of onion powder

- Salt and pepper, to taste

- 1/2 cup of non-fat Greek yogurt

- 2 tablespoons crumbled blue cheese

- 1 tablespoon lemon juice

- 1/4 teaspoon of garlic powder

- Salt and pepper, to taste

- Bamboo skewers, soaked in water for 30 minutes

Instructions List:

1. In a bowl, combine hot sauce, olive oil, honey, garlic powder, onion powder, salt, and pepper. Add chicken cubes to the bowl and toss until evenly coated. Let marinate for at least 10 minutes.

2. Preheat grill or grill pan over medium-high heat.

3. Thread marinated chicken cubes onto bamboo skewers.

4. Grill skewers for 6-8 minutes per side, or until chicken is cooked through and slightly charred.

5. In another bowl, mix together Greek yogurt, crumbled blue cheese, lemon juice, garlic powder, salt, and pepper to make the dipping sauce.

6. Serve hot chicken skewers with blue cheese dipping sauce on the side.

7. Enjoy!

Nutritional Information (per serving):

- Calories: 220

- Protein: 30g

- Total Fats: 6g

- Fiber: 0g

- Carbohydrates: 10g

Points: 0 Points

Slow Cooker Cider-Braised Pulled Chicken Sandwiches

Time to Prepare: 10 minutes
Cooking Time: 6 hours
Number of Servings: 6

Ingredients:

- 2 lbs boneless, skinless chicken breasts

- 1 cup of apple cider vinegar

- 1 cup of unsweetened apple cider

- 1/4 cup of Worcestershire sauce

- 2 tablespoons honey

- 1 tablespoon Dijon mustard

- 1 teaspoon of smoked paprika

- 1 teaspoon of garlic powder

- 1/2 teaspoon of onion powder

- Salt and pepper, to taste

- 6 whole wheat sandwich buns

- Optional toppings: sliced apples, shredded cabbage

Instructions List:

1. Place chicken breasts in the slow cooker.

2. In a mixing bowl, whisk together apple cider vinegar, apple cider, Worcestershire sauce, honey, Dijon mustard, smoked paprika, garlic powder, onion powder, salt, and pepper.

3. Pour the mixture over the chicken breasts in the slow cooker.

4. Cover and cook on low for 6 hours, or until the chicken is tender and easily shreds with a fork.

5. Once cooked, remove the chicken from the slow cooker and shred it using two forks.

6. Return the shredded chicken to the slow cooker and mix it with the cooking liquid.

7. Toast the whole wheat sandwich buns if desired.

8. Serve the pulled chicken on the buns, topped with optional sliced apples and shredded cabbage.

9. Enjoy!

Nutritional Information (per serving):

- Calories: 280

- Protein: 32g

- Total Fats: 4g

- Fiber: 4g

- Carbohydrates: 28g

Points: 0 Points

Orange-Glazed Turkey Cutlets

Time to Prepare: 10 minutes
Cooking Time: 15 minutes
Number of Servings: 4

Ingredients:

- 4 turkey cutlets

- Salt and pepper, to taste

- 1 tablespoon olive oil

- 1/4 cup of orange juice

- 2 tablespoons honey

- 1 tablespoon low-sodium soy sauce

- 1 teaspoon of grated fresh ginger

- 1 teaspoon of cornstarch

- 1 tablespoon water

- Optional garnish: chopped fresh parsley

Instructions List:

1. Season the turkey cutlets with salt and pepper on both sides.

2. In a large skillet, heat olive oil over medium-high heat.

3. Add the turkey cutlets to the skillet and cook for 3-4 minutes per side, or until golden brown and cooked through.

4. In a small bowl, whisk together orange juice, honey, soy sauce, and grated ginger.

5. In another small bowl, mix cornstarch with water to make a slurry.

6. Pour the orange juice mixture into the skillet with the turkey cutlets.

7. Stir in the cornstarch slurry and bring the mixture to a simmer.

8. Cook for 2-3 minutes, or until the sauce thickens and coats the back of a spoon.

9. Remove the skillet from heat and let the turkey cutlets rest in the sauce for a minute.

10. Serve the turkey cutlets with the orange glaze spooned over the top.

11. Garnish with chopped fresh parsley if desired.

12. Enjoy!

Nutritional Information (per serving):

- Calories: 240

- Protein: 28g

- Total Fats: 6g

- Fiber: 0g

- Carbohydrates: 18g

Points: 4 Points

Pesto Stuffed Chicken Breast

Time to Prepare: 15 minutes
Cooking Time: 25 minutes
Number of Servings: 4

Ingredients:

- 4 boneless, skinless chicken breasts

- Salt and pepper, to taste

- 1/4 cup of prepared pesto sauce

- 1/2 cup of shredded mozzarella cheese

- 1 tablespoon olive oil

Instructions List:

1. Preheat the oven to 375°F (190°C).

2. Using a sharp knife, make a horizontal slit along the side of each chicken breast to form a pocket, being careful not to cut all the way through.

3. Season the inside of each chicken breast with salt and pepper.

4. Spoon pesto sauce into each chicken breast pocket, dividing it evenly among them.

5. Sprinkle shredded mozzarella cheese into each chicken breast pocket, also dividing it evenly.

6. Close the pockets by pressing the edges together.

7. Heat olive oil in an oven-safe skillet over medium-high heat.

8. Sear the stuffed chicken breasts in the skillet for 2-3 minutes on each side, until golden brown.

9. Transfer the skillet to the preheated oven and bake for 18-20 minutes, or until the chicken is cooked through and no longer pink in the center.

10. Remove the skillet from the oven and let the chicken rest for a few minutes before serving.

11. Serve the pesto stuffed chicken breasts hot.

12. Enjoy!

Nutritional Information (per serving):

- Calories: 320
- Protein: 36g
- Total Fats: 17g
- Fiber: 1g
- Carbohydrates: 2g

Points: 5 Points

BBQ Chicken Lettuce Wraps

Time to Prepare: 15 minutes
Cooking Time: 15 minutes
Number of Servings: 4

Ingredients:

- 1 lb boneless, skinless chicken breasts, diced
- Salt and pepper, to taste
- 1/2 cup of BBQ sauce
- 1 tablespoon olive oil
- 1/2 red onion, diced
- 1 bell pepper, diced
- 1/2 cup of corn kernels
- 1/2 cup of black beans, drained and rinsed
- 1/4 cup of chopped fresh cilantro
- 1 head iceberg or butter lettuce, leaves separated
- Optional toppings: diced tomatoes, avocado slices, shredded cheese

Instructions List:

1. Season the diced chicken breasts with salt and pepper.
2. Heat olive oil in a skillet over medium-high heat.
3. Add the seasoned chicken to the skillet and cook for 6-8 minutes, or until cooked through.
4. Pour BBQ sauce over the cooked chicken and stir to coat evenly. Cook for an additional 2-3 minutes.
5. In a separate skillet, sauté the diced red onion and bell pepper until softened, about 5 minutes.
6. Add corn kernels and black beans to the skillet with the onion and bell pepper, and cook for another 2-3 minutes.
7. To assemble the lettuce wraps, spoon some of the BBQ chicken mixture onto each lettuce leaf.
8. Top with the sautéed vegetable mixture and chopped cilantro.
9. Add any optional toppings as desired.

10. Serve the BBQ chicken lettuce wraps immediately.

11. Enjoy!

Nutritional Information (per serving):

- Calories: 280

- Protein: 25g

- Total Fats: 8g

- Fiber: 4g

- Carbohydrates: 28g

Points: 3 Points

Thai Basil Chicken Stir-Fry

Time to Prepare: 15 minutes
Cooking Time: 15 minutes
Number of Servings: 4

Ingredients:

- 1 lb boneless, skinless chicken breasts, thinly sliced

- 2 tablespoons soy sauce

- 1 tablespoon oyster sauce

- 1 tablespoon fish sauce

- 1 tablespoon brown sugar

- 2 tablespoons vegetable oil

- 4 cloves garlic, minced

- 1 red bell pepper, thinly sliced

- 1 yellow bell pepper, thinly sliced

- 1 onion, thinly sliced

- 1 cup of fresh basil leaves

- Cooked rice, for serving

Instructions List:

1. In a small bowl, mix together soy sauce, oyster sauce, fish sauce, and brown sugar. Set aside.

2. Heat vegetable oil in a large skillet or wok over medium-high heat.

3. Add minced garlic to the skillet and cook for 1 minute until fragrant.

4. Add sliced chicken to the skillet and stir-fry until cooked through, about 5-6 minutes.

5. Push the chicken to one side of the skillet and add sliced bell peppers and onion to the other side. Stir-fry until vegetables are tender-crisp, about 3-4 minutes.

6. Pour the sauce mixture over the chicken and vegetables in the skillet. Stir to combine and coat everything evenly.

7. Add fresh basil leaves to the skillet and toss until wilted, about 1 minute.

8. Remove from heat and serve the Thai basil chicken stir-fry hot over cooked rice.

9. Enjoy!

Nutritional Information (per serving):

- Calories: 280
- Protein: 28g
- Total Fats: 11g
- Fiber: 3g
- Carbohydrates: 16g

Points: 5 Points

Chapter 5: Beans & Grains

Black Bean Quinoa Salad

Time to Prepare: 15 minutes
Cooking Time: 15 minutes
Number of Servings: 4

Ingredients:

- 1 cup of quinoa, rinsed
- 2 cups of water
- 1 (15 oz) can black beans, drained and rinsed
- 1 cup of cherry tomatoes, halved
- 1/2 cup of red onion, finely chopped
- 1/2 cup of cucumber, diced
- 1/4 cup of fresh cilantro, chopped
- 2 tablespoons lime juice
- 2 tablespoons olive oil
- 1 teaspoon of ground cumin
- Salt and pepper, to taste
- Avocado slices, for garnish (optional)

Instructions List:

1. In a medium saucepan, bring the water to a boil. Add quinoa, reduce heat to low, cover, and simmer for 15 minutes or until quinoa is cooked and water is absorbed. Remove from heat and let it cool.
2. In a large mixing bowl, combine cooked quinoa, black beans, cherry tomatoes, red onion, cucumber, and cilantro.
3. In a small bowl, whisk together lime juice, olive oil, ground cumin, salt, and pepper to make the dressing.
4. Pour the dressing over the quinoa mixture and toss until everything is evenly coated.
5. Taste and adjust seasoning if needed.
6. Garnish with avocado slices, if desired.
7. Serve chilled or at room temperature.
8. Enjoy!

Nutritional Information (per serving):

- Calories: 325
- Protein: 12g
- Total Fats: 8g
- Fiber: 10g

- Carbohydrates: 52g

Points: 4 Points

Chickpea and Spinach Stew

Time to Prepare: 10 minutes
Cooking Time: 25 minutes
Number of Servings: 4

Ingredients:

- 1 tablespoon olive oil
- 1 onion, chopped
- 3 cloves garlic, minced
- 1 teaspoon of ground cumin
- 1 teaspoon of ground coriander
- 1/2 teaspoon of paprika
- 1/4 teaspoon of cayenne pepper (optional)
- 1 (15 oz) can chickpeas, drained and rinsed
- 1 (14.5 oz) can diced tomatoes
- 4 cups fresh spinach leaves
- Salt and pepper, to taste
- 2 cups of vegetable broth
- Fresh parsley, for garnish (optional)

Instructions List:

1. Heat olive oil in a large pot over medium heat. Add chopped onion and cook until softened, about 5 minutes.

2. Add minced garlic, ground cumin, ground coriander, paprika, and cayenne pepper (if using). Cook for another 1-2 minutes until fragrant.

3. Stir in chickpeas and diced tomatoes. Season with salt and pepper.

4. Pour in vegetable broth and bring the mixture to a simmer.

5. Reduce heat to low and let the stew simmer for 15 minutes, stirring occasionally.

6. Add fresh spinach leaves to the pot and cook until wilted, about 3-5 minutes.

7. Taste and adjust seasoning if necessary.

8. Serve hot, garnished with fresh parsley if desired.

Nutritional Information (per serving):

- Calories: 227
- Protein: 10g

- Total Fats: 5g

- Fiber: 8g

- Carbohydrates: 36g

Points: 5 Points

Mexican Rice Bowl

Time to Prepare: 10 minutes
Cooking Time: 20 minutes
Number of Servings: 4

Ingredients:

- 1 cup of brown rice

- 1 tablespoon olive oil

- 1 onion, diced

- 2 cloves garlic, minced

- 1 red bell pepper, diced

- 1 cup of corn kernels (fresh or frozen)

- 1 (15 oz) can black beans, drained and rinsed

- 1 (14.5 oz) can diced tomatoes

- 1 teaspoon of chili powder

- 1/2 teaspoon of ground cumin

- Salt and pepper, to taste

- Fresh cilantro, for garnish (optional)

- Avocado slices, for garnish (optional)

- Lime wedges, for serving

Instructions List:

1. Cook brown rice according to package instructions.

2. In a large skillet, heat olive oil over medium heat. Add diced onion and cook until translucent, about 5 minutes.

3. Add minced garlic and cook for another 1-2 minutes until fragrant.

4. Stir in diced red bell pepper and corn kernels. Cook for 5-7 minutes until vegetables are tender.

5. Add drained black beans, diced tomatoes, chili powder, and ground cumin to the skillet. Season with salt and pepper.

6. Let the mixture simmer for 5-7 minutes, stirring occasionally.

7. To assemble the bowls, divide cooked brown rice among serving bowls. Top with the black bean and vegetable mixture.

8. Garnish with fresh cilantro and avocado slices if desired. Serve with lime wedges on the side.

Nutritional Information (per serving):

- Calories: 356

- Protein: 12g

- Total Fats: 7g

- Fiber: 10g

- Carbohydrates: 64g

Points: 6 Points

Italian Chicken Soup with Vegetables

Time to Prepare: 15 minutes
Cooking Time: 25 minutes
Number of Servings: 6

Ingredients:

- 1 tablespoon olive oil

- 1 onion, chopped

- 2 cloves garlic, minced

- 2 carrots, diced

- 2 celery stalks, diced

- 1 zucchini, diced

- 1 yellow squash, diced

- 1 teaspoon of dried basil

- 1 teaspoon of dried oregano

- 1/2 teaspoon of dried thyme

- Salt and pepper, to taste

- 6 cups chicken broth

- 1 (14.5 oz) can diced tomatoes

- 2 cups of shredded cooked chicken breast

- 2 cups of chopped kale or spinach

- Fresh parsley, for garnish (optional)

- Grated Parmesan cheese, for serving (optional)

Instructions List:

1. In a large pot, heat olive oil over medium heat. Add chopped onion and cook until translucent, about 5 minutes.

2. Add minced garlic and cook for another 1-2 minutes until fragrant.

3. Stir in diced carrots, celery, zucchini, and yellow squash. Cook for 5-7 minutes until vegetables start to soften.

4. Add dried basil, dried oregano, dried thyme, salt, and pepper to the pot. Stir to combine.

5. Pour in chicken broth and diced tomatoes with their juices. Bring to a simmer.

6. Add shredded cooked chicken breast and chopped kale or spinach to the pot. Simmer for an additional 10-15 minutes until vegetables are tender and flavors are well mixed.

7. Taste and adjust seasoning if needed.

8. Serve hot, garnished with fresh parsley and grated Parmesan cheese if desired.

Nutritional Information (per serving):

- Calories: 189

- Protein: 18g

- Total Fats: 6g

- Fiber: 4g

- Carbohydrates: 15g

Points: 0 Points

Mediterranean Chickpea Salad

Time to Prepare: 15 minutes
Cooking Time: 0 minutes
Number of Servings: 4

Ingredients:

- 2 (15 oz) cans chickpeas, drained and rinsed

- 1 cucumber, diced

- 1 red bell pepper, diced

- 1/2 red onion, finely chopped

- 1 cup of cherry tomatoes, halved

- 1/4 cup of chopped fresh parsley

- 1/4 cup of chopped fresh mint

- 1/4 cup of crumbled feta cheese (optional)

- 2 tablespoons extra virgin olive oil

- 2 tablespoons red wine vinegar

- Juice of 1 lemon

- Salt and pepper, to taste

Instructions List:

1. In a large mixing bowl, combine chickpeas, diced cucumber, diced red bell pepper, finely chopped red onion, halved cherry tomatoes, chopped fresh parsley, and chopped fresh mint.

2. If using, add crumbled feta cheese to the bowl.

3. Drizzle extra virgin olive oil, red wine vinegar, and lemon juice over the salad ingredients.

4. Season with salt and pepper to taste.

5. Gently toss everything together until well mixed.

6. Serve immediately or refrigerate for at least 30 minutes to allow the flavors to meld before serving.

Nutritional Information (per serving):

- Calories: 310

- Protein: 11g

- Total Fats: 11g

- Fiber: 10g

- Carbohydrates: 43g

Points: 0 Points

Quinoa-Stuffed Bell Peppers

Time to Prepare: 20 minutes
Cooking Time: 40 minutes
Number of Servings: 4

Ingredients:

- 4 large bell peppers, any color

- 1 cup of quinoa, rinsed

- 2 cups of vegetable broth

- 1 can (15 oz) black beans, drained and rinsed

- 1 cup of corn kernels (fresh, canned, or frozen)

- 1 cup of diced tomatoes

- 1/2 cup of diced onion

- 2 cloves garlic, minced

- 1 teaspoon of ground cumin

- 1 teaspoon of chili powder

- Salt and pepper, to taste

- 1/4 cup of chopped fresh cilantro (optional)

- 1/4 cup of shredded cheese (optional, for topping)

Instructions List:

1. Preheat the oven to 375°F (190°C).

2. Cut the tops off the bell peppers and remove the seeds and membranes.

3. In a medium saucepan, combine quinoa and vegetable broth. Bring to a boil, then reduce heat, cover, and simmer for about 15 minutes, or until quinoa is cooked and liquid is absorbed.

4. In a large mixing bowl, combine cooked quinoa, black beans, corn kernels, diced tomatoes, diced onion, minced garlic, ground cumin, chili powder, salt, and pepper. Stir well to combine.

5. Stuff each bell pepper with the quinoa mixture, packing it in tightly.

6. Place the stuffed bell peppers in a baking dish. If desired, sprinkle shredded cheese on top of each pepper.

7. Cover the baking dish with foil and bake in the preheated oven for 30 minutes.

8. Remove the foil and bake for an additional 10 minutes, or until the peppers are tender and the filling is heated through.

9. Garnish with chopped fresh cilantro, if desired, before serving.

Nutritional Information (per serving):

*   Calories: 367

*   Protein: 14g

*   Total Fats: 4g

*   Fiber: 12g

*   Carbohydrates: 70g

Points: 0 Points

Farro Salad with Roasted Vegetables

Time to Prepare: 15 minutes
Cooking Time: 25 minutes
Number of Servings: 4

Ingredients:

*   1 cup of farro

*   2 cups of water

*   2 cups of mixed vegetables (such as bell peppers, zucchini, cherry tomatoes)

*   2 tablespoons olive oil

*   Salt and pepper, to taste

*   2 tablespoons balsamic vinegar

*   1 tablespoon honey

*   2 cloves garlic, minced

*   1/4 cup of chopped fresh basil

*   1/4 cup of crumbled feta cheese (optional)

Instructions List:

1. Preheat the oven to 400°F (200°C).

2. Rinse the farro under cold water. In a medium saucepan, combine farro and water. Bring to a boil, then reduce heat, cover, and simmer for about 20-25 minutes, or until farro is tender. Drain any excess water and let it cool.

3. Meanwhile, prepare the vegetables. Cut them into bite-sized pieces and place them on a baking sheet. Drizzle with olive oil and season with salt and pepper. Toss to coat evenly.

4. Roast the vegetables in the preheated oven for 20-25 minutes, or until they are tender and slightly caramelized.

5. In a small bowl, whisk together balsamic vinegar, honey, minced garlic, and a pinch of salt and pepper to make the dressing.

6. In a large mixing bowl, combine cooked farro, roasted vegetables, chopped fresh basil, and the prepared dressing. Toss until everything is well coated.

7. If desired, sprinkle crumbled feta cheese over the salad before serving.

Nutritional Information (per serving):

*   Calories: 292

*   Protein: 7g

*   Total Fats: 8g

*   Fiber: 7g

*   Carbohydrates: 50g

Points: 4 Points

Wild Rice Pilaf

Time to Prepare: 10 minutes
Cooking Time: 45 minutes
Number of Servings: 6

Ingredients:

*   1 cup of wild rice

*   2 cups of low-sodium chicken or vegetable broth

*   1 tablespoon olive oil

*   1 small onion, finely chopped

*   2 cloves garlic, minced

*   1/2 cup of diced carrots

*   1/2 cup of diced celery

*   1/2 cup of sliced mushrooms

*   Salt and pepper, to taste

- 1/4 cup of chopped fresh parsley

- 1/4 cup of chopped almonds (optional)

Instructions List:

1. Rinse the wild rice under cold water. In a medium saucepan, combine the wild rice and chicken or vegetable broth. Bring to a boil, then reduce heat, cover, and simmer for about 40-45 minutes, or until the rice is tender and the liquid is absorbed. Remove from heat and let it sit, covered, for 5 minutes.

2. In a large skillet, heat olive oil over medium heat. Add the chopped onion and garlic, and cook until softened, about 3-4 minutes.

3. Add the diced carrots, celery, and sliced mushrooms to the skillet. Cook, stirring occasionally, until the vegetables are tender, about 5-6 minutes.

4. Once the wild rice is cooked, fluff it with a fork and transfer it to the skillet with the cooked vegetables. Stir to combine.

5. Season the pilaf with salt and pepper to taste. If desired, stir in chopped fresh parsley and chopped almonds.

6. Serve the wild rice pilaf hot as a side dish or as a main course.

Nutritional Information (per serving):

- Calories: 185

- Protein: 5g

- Total Fats: 4g

- Fiber: 3g

- Carbohydrates: 32g

Points: 5 Points

Barley and Mushroom Risotto

Time to Prepare: 10 minutes
Cooking Time: 40 minutes
Number of Servings: 4

Ingredients:

- 1 cup of pearl barley

- 4 cups low-sodium vegetable broth

- 1 tablespoon olive oil

- 1 onion, finely chopped

- 2 cloves garlic, minced

- 8 ounces mushrooms (such as cremini or button), sliced

- 1/4 cup of dry white wine (optional)

- Salt and pepper, to taste

- 1/4 cup of grated Parmesan cheese

- 2 tablespoons chopped fresh parsley

Instructions List:

1. In a medium saucepan, bring the vegetable broth to a simmer over medium heat.

2. In a separate large skillet, heat the olive oil over medium heat. Add the chopped onion and cook until softened, about 3-4 minutes. Add the minced garlic and cook for an additional minute.

3. Add the sliced mushrooms to the skillet and cook until they release their moisture and start to brown, about 5-6 minutes.

4. Stir in the pearl barley and cook for 1-2 minutes, until lightly toasted.

5. If using, pour in the dry white wine and cook until it is absorbed by the barley, stirring constantly.

6. Ladle in 1 cup of the warm vegetable broth into the skillet with the barley mixture. Cook, stirring frequently, until the broth is absorbed. Continue adding the broth, 1 cup of at a time, stirring frequently and allowing each addition to be absorbed before adding more, until the barley is tender and creamy, about 30-35 minutes.

7. Once the barley is cooked to your desired consistency, season the risotto with salt and pepper to taste.

8. Remove the skillet from the heat and stir in the grated Parmesan cheese until melted and well mixed.

9. Serve the barley and mushroom risotto hot, garnished with chopped fresh parsley.

Nutritional Information (per serving):

- Calories: 281

- Protein: 9g

- Total Fats: 6g

- Fiber: 9g

- Carbohydrates: 48g

Points: 6 Points

Edamame and Brown Rice Stir-Fry

Time to Prepare: 10 minutes
Cooking Time: 20 minutes
Number of Servings: 4

Ingredients:

- 2 cups of cooked brown rice

- 2 cups of shelled edamame, cooked

- 1 tablespoon sesame oil

- 1 onion, diced

- 2 cloves garlic, minced

- 1 red bell pepper, diced

- 1 carrot, julienned

- 1 cup of snow peas, trimmed

- 2 tablespoons low-sodium soy sauce

- 1 tablespoon rice vinegar

- 1 tablespoon honey or maple syrup

- 1 teaspoon of grated fresh ginger

- Sesame seeds, for garnish

- Chopped green onions, for garnish

Instructions List:

1. In a large skillet or wok, heat the sesame oil over medium heat. Add the diced onion and minced garlic, and cook until softened, about 2-3 minutes.

2. Add the diced red bell pepper, julienned carrot, and snow peas to the skillet. Cook, stirring frequently, until the vegetables are tender-crisp, about 5-6 minutes.

3. Stir in the cooked brown rice and shelled edamame, and cook for an additional 2-3 minutes to heat through.

4. In a small bowl, whisk together the low-sodium soy sauce, rice vinegar, honey or maple syrup, and grated fresh ginger.

5. Pour the sauce over the rice and vegetable mixture in the skillet. Stir well to coat everything evenly with the sauce.

6. Cook for another 2-3 minutes, until the sauce has thickened slightly and everything is heated through.

7. Remove the skillet from the heat and transfer the stir-fry to serving plates.

8. Garnish with sesame seeds and chopped green onions before serving.

Nutritional Information (per serving):

- Calories: 292

- Protein: 14g

- Total Fats: 7g

- Fiber: 9g

- Carbohydrates: 45g

Points: 4 Points

Red Lentil Soup

Time to Prepare: 10 minutes
Cooking Time: 25 minutes
Number of Servings: 6

Ingredients:

- 1 tablespoon olive oil

- 1 onion, diced

- 2 carrots, diced

- 2 celery stalks, diced

- 3 cloves garlic, minced

- 1 cup of dried red lentils, rinsed and drained

- 1 can (14 oz) diced tomatoes

- 4 cups vegetable broth

- 1 teaspoon of ground cumin

- 1 teaspoon of ground coriander

- 1/2 teaspoon of smoked paprika

- Salt and pepper, to taste

- Fresh cilantro or parsley, for garnish

Instructions List:

1. In a large pot, heat the olive oil over medium heat. Add the diced onion, carrots, and celery. Cook, stirring occasionally, until the vegetables are softened, about 5-6 minutes.

2. Add the minced garlic to the pot and cook for an additional 1-2 minutes, until fragrant.

3. Stir in the rinsed and drained red lentils, diced tomatoes, vegetable broth, ground cumin, ground coriander, and smoked paprika.

4. Bring the soup to a boil, then reduce the heat to low. Cover and simmer for 15-20 minutes, or until the lentils are tender.

5. Once the lentils are cooked, use an immersion blender to blend the soup until smooth. Alternatively, you can transfer the soup to a blender in batches and blend until smooth.

6. Season the soup with salt and pepper, to taste.

7. Ladle the soup into bowls and garnish with fresh cilantro or parsley before serving.

Nutritional Information (per serving):

- Calories: 192

- Protein: 10g

- Total Fats: 3g

- Fiber: 8g

- Carbohydrates: 31g

Points: 3 Points

Chapter 6: Meat

Beef and Broccoli Stir-Fry

Time to Prepare: 15 minutes
Cooking Time: 15 minutes
Number of Servings: 4

Ingredients:

- 1 lb flank steak, thinly sliced against the grain
- 1/4 cup of low-sodium soy sauce
- 2 tablespoons hoisin sauce
- 2 tablespoons oyster sauce
- 2 cloves garlic, minced
- 1 teaspoon of grated ginger
- 1 tablespoon cornstarch
- 2 tablespoons vegetable oil, divided
- 1 head broccoli, cut into florets
- 1 red bell pepper, sliced
- 1 yellow bell pepper, sliced
- Cooked brown rice, for serving
- Sesame seeds, for garnish (optional)
- Sliced green onions, for garnish (optional)

Instructions List:

1. In a bowl, combine the thinly sliced flank steak with low-sodium soy sauce, hoisin sauce, oyster sauce, minced garlic, grated ginger, and cornstarch. Toss until the steak is evenly coated. Let it marinate for at least 15 minutes.

2. Heat 1 tablespoon of vegetable oil in a large skillet or wok over high heat. Add the marinated steak and stir-fry for 2-3 minutes until browned. Remove the steak from the skillet and set aside.

3. In the same skillet, add the remaining tablespoon of vegetable oil. Add the broccoli florets and sliced bell peppers. Stir-fry for 3-4 minutes until the vegetables are tender-crisp.

4. Return the cooked steak to the skillet and toss with the vegetables until heated through.

5. Serve the beef and broccoli stir-fry hot over cooked brown rice.

6. Garnish with sesame seeds and sliced green onions, if desired.

Nutritional Information (per serving):

- Calories: 335
- Protein: 27g
- Total Fats: 14g

- Fiber: 5g

- Carbohydrates: 26g

Points: 5 Points

Italian Meatball Subs

Time to Prepare: 20 minutes
Cooking Time: 25 minutes
Number of Servings: 4

Ingredients:

- 1 lb lean ground beef

- 1/2 cup of breadcrumbs

- 1/4 cup of grated Parmesan cheese

- 1 egg

- 2 cloves garlic, minced

- 1 teaspoon of dried oregano

- 1 teaspoon of dried basil

- Salt and pepper, to taste

- 1 tablespoon olive oil

- 1 jar (24 oz) marinara sauce

- 4 whole wheat hoagie rolls

- 1 cup of shredded mozzarella cheese

- Fresh basil leaves, for garnish (optional)

Instructions List:

1. Preheat the oven to 375°F (190°C).

2. In a large bowl, combine the lean ground beef, breadcrumbs, grated Parmesan cheese, egg, minced garlic, dried oregano, dried basil, salt, and pepper. Mix until well mixed.

3. Shape the mixture into meatballs, about 1 inch in diameter.

4. Heat olive oil in a large skillet over medium heat. Add the meatballs and cook until browned on all sides, about 5-7 minutes.

5. Pour marinara sauce into the skillet with the meatballs. Stir to coat the meatballs evenly with the sauce.

6. Transfer the skillet to the preheated oven and bake for 15 minutes, or until the meatballs are cooked through.

7. While the meatballs are baking, split the hoagie rolls and place them on a baking sheet. Toast them in the oven for about 5 minutes.

8. Remove the meatballs from the oven. Place 3-4 meatballs inside each toasted hoagie roll.

9. Sprinkle shredded mozzarella cheese over the meatballs in each roll.

10. Return the baking sheet to the oven and bake for an additional 5 minutes, or until the cheese is melted and bubbly.

11. Garnish with fresh basil leaves, if desired, before serving.

Nutritional Information (per serving):

- Calories: 522

- Protein: 34g

- Total Fats: 19g

- Fiber: 6g

- Carbohydrates: 53g

Points: 6 Points

Pork Tenderloin with Apple Chutney

Time to Prepare: 15 minutes
Cooking Time: 25 minutes
Number of Servings: 4

Ingredients:

- 1 lb pork tenderloin

- Salt and pepper, to taste

- 1 tablespoon olive oil

- 2 apples, peeled, cored, and chopped

- 1/4 cup of diced onion

- 2 tablespoons apple cider vinegar

- 2 tablespoons brown sugar

- 1/4 teaspoon of ground cinnamon

- 1/4 teaspoon of ground ginger

- 1/4 teaspoon of ground cloves

Instructions List:

1. Preheat the oven to 400°F (200°C).

2. Season the pork tenderloin with salt and pepper.

3. Heat olive oil in an oven-safe skillet over medium-high heat. Add the pork tenderloin and sear on all sides until browned, about 3-4 minutes per side.

4. Transfer the skillet to the preheated oven and roast the pork tenderloin for 15-20 minutes, or until the internal temperature reaches 145°F (63°C).

5. While the pork is roasting, prepare the apple chutney. In a saucepan, combine the chopped apples, diced onion, apple cider vinegar, brown sugar, ground cinnamon, ground ginger, and ground cloves.

6. Bring the mixture to a simmer over medium heat. Cook, stirring occasionally, until the apples are softened and the mixture has thickened slightly, about 10-12 minutes.

7. Once the pork tenderloin is done, remove it from the oven and let it rest for a few minutes before slicing.

8. Serve the sliced pork tenderloin with the apple chutney on top.

Nutritional Information (per serving):

- Calories: 286

- Protein: 27g

- Total Fats: 8g

- Fiber: 3g

- Carbohydrates: 25g

Points: 4 Points

Korean BBQ Beef Lettuce Wraps

Time to Prepare: 15 minutes
Cooking Time: 15 minutes
Number of Servings: 4

Ingredients:

- 1 lb lean beef (such as sirloin or flank steak), thinly sliced

- 1/4 cup of low-sodium soy sauce

- 2 tablespoons brown sugar

- 2 tablespoons rice vinegar

- 2 cloves garlic, minced

- 1 teaspoon of grated fresh ginger

- 1 tablespoon sesame oil

- 1 tablespoon vegetable oil

- 1 onion, thinly sliced

- 1 bell pepper, thinly sliced

- 1/4 cup of chopped green onions

- 1 head butter lettuce, leaves separated

- Optional toppings: sliced cucumber, shredded carrots, sesame seeds

Instructions List:

1. In a bowl, whisk together the soy sauce, brown sugar, rice vinegar, minced garlic, grated ginger, and sesame oil to make the marinade.

2. Place the thinly sliced beef in a shallow dish or a resealable plastic bag. Pour the marinade over the beef, making sure it's well coated. Marinate in the refrigerator for at least 30 minutes, or up to 2 hours.

3. Heat vegetable oil in a large skillet or wok over medium-high heat. Add the sliced onion and bell pepper, and stir-fry for 2-3 minutes until they start to soften.

4. Add the marinated beef to the skillet, reserving any excess marinade. Stir-fry for 4-5 minutes until the beef is cooked through.

5. Pour the reserved marinade into the skillet and cook for an additional 1-2 minutes, stirring occasionally, until the sauce thickens slightly.

6. Remove the skillet from the heat and stir in the chopped green onions.

7. To serve, spoon the Korean BBQ beef mixture into individual lettuce leaves. Top with optional toppings like sliced cucumber, shredded carrots, and sesame seeds if desired.

Nutritional Information (per serving):

- Calories: 295

- Protein: 27g

- Total Fats: 12g

- Fiber: 3g

- Carbohydrates: 17g

Points: 5 Points

Turkey and Black Bean Chili

Time to Prepare: 15 minutes
Cooking Time: 30 minutes
Number of Servings: 6

Ingredients:

- 1 lb lean ground turkey

- 1 onion, diced

- 3 cloves garlic, minced

- 1 bell pepper, diced

- 1 can (15 oz) black beans, drained and rinsed

- 1 can (14.5 oz) diced tomatoes

- 1 cup of low-sodium chicken broth

- 2 tablespoons tomato paste

- 1 tablespoon chili powder

- 1 teaspoon of ground cumin

- 1 teaspoon of paprika

- Salt and pepper, to taste

- Optional toppings: chopped cilantro, sliced green onions, shredded cheese, Greek yogurt

Instructions List:

1. In a large pot or Dutch oven, cook the ground turkey over medium heat until browned, breaking it up with a spoon as it cooks.

2. Add the diced onion, minced garlic, and diced bell pepper to the pot. Cook for 3-4 minutes until the vegetables are softened.

3. Stir in the black beans, diced tomatoes, chicken broth, tomato paste, chili powder, ground cumin, and paprika.

4. Season with salt and pepper to taste.

5. Bring the chili to a simmer, then reduce the heat to low. Cover and let it simmer for 20-25 minutes, stirring occasionally, until flavors are blended and chili has thickened.

6. Serve hot, garnished with optional toppings like chopped cilantro, sliced green onions, shredded cheese, and Greek yogurt if desired.

Nutritional Information (per serving):

- Calories: 250
- Protein: 22g
- Total Fats: 6g
- Fiber: 8g
- Carbohydrates: 27g

Points: 0 Points

Beef and Broccoli Stir-Fry

Time to Prepare: 15 minutes
Cooking Time: 15 minutes
Number of Servings: 4

Ingredients:

- 1 lb lean beef steak, thinly sliced
- 4 cups broccoli florets
- 1 onion, thinly sliced
- 3 cloves garlic, minced
- 1/4 cup of low-sodium soy sauce
- 2 tablespoons oyster sauce
- 1 tablespoon sesame oil
- 1 tablespoon cornstarch
- 1 teaspoon of grated ginger
- 1 teaspoon of honey
- Salt and pepper, to taste
- Optional garnish: sliced green onions, sesame seeds

Instructions List:

1. In a small bowl, whisk together the soy sauce, oyster sauce, sesame oil, cornstarch, grated ginger, and honey to make the sauce. Set aside.

2. Heat a large skillet or wok over medium-high heat. Add the thinly sliced beef and cook until browned, about 2-3 minutes per side. Remove the beef from the skillet and set aside.

3. In the same skillet, add the sliced onion and minced garlic. Cook for 2-3 minutes until softened.

4. Add the broccoli florets to the skillet and cook for an additional 3-4 minutes until they begin to soften.

5. Return the cooked beef to the skillet and pour the prepared sauce over the beef and broccoli. Stir well to combine.

6. Cook for another 2-3 minutes until the sauce has thickened and everything is heated through.

7. Serve hot, garnished with sliced green onions and sesame seeds if desired.

Nutritional Information (per serving):

- Calories: 280
- Protein: 28g
- Total Fats: 9g
- Fiber: 4g
- Carbohydrates: 22g

Points: 0 Points

Balsamic Glazed Pork Chops

Time to Prepare: 10 minutes
Cooking Time: 20 minutes
Number of Servings: 4

Ingredients:

- 4 boneless pork chops
- Salt and pepper, to taste
- 2 tablespoons olive oil
- 1/4 cup of balsamic vinegar
- 2 tablespoons honey
- 2 cloves garlic, minced
- 1 teaspoon of dried thyme
- 1 teaspoon of dried rosemary

Instructions List:

1. Season the pork chops with salt and pepper on both sides.

2. Heat olive oil in a large skillet over medium-high heat. Add the pork chops and cook for 4-5 minutes on each side until browned and cooked through. Remove the pork chops from the skillet and set aside.

3. In the same skillet, add balsamic vinegar, honey, minced garlic, dried thyme, and dried rosemary. Cook for 2-3 minutes, stirring constantly, until the sauce thickens slightly.

4. Return the pork chops to the skillet, spooning the glaze over them. Cook for an additional 1-2 minutes to heat through and coat the pork chops with the glaze.

5. Serve hot, garnished with fresh herbs if desired.

Nutritional Information (per serving):

- Calories: 280

- Protein: 24g

- Total Fats: 14g

- Fiber: 0g

- Carbohydrates: 12g

Points: 4 Points

Jamaican Jerk Chicken

Time to Prepare: 15 minutes
Cooking Time: 25 minutes
Number of Servings: 4

Ingredients:

- 4 boneless, skinless chicken breasts

- 2 tablespoons olive oil

- 3 tablespoons Jamaican jerk seasoning

- 2 tablespoons soy sauce

- 2 tablespoons lime juice

- 2 cloves garlic, minced

- 1 teaspoon of brown sugar

- Salt and pepper, to taste

Instructions List:

1. In a bowl, mix together olive oil, Jamaican jerk seasoning, soy sauce, lime juice, minced garlic, brown sugar, salt, and pepper.

2. Add the chicken breasts to the marinade, ensuring they are evenly coated. Marinate in the refrigerator for at least 1 hour, or overnight for best results.

3. Preheat the grill or grill pan to medium-high heat.

4. Remove the chicken breasts from the marinade and discard any excess marinade.

5. Grill the chicken breasts for 6-7 minutes on each side, or until fully cooked through and charred on the outside.

6. Remove from the grill and let rest for a few minutes before serving.

7. Serve hot with your favorite side dishes.

Nutritional Information (per serving):

- Calories: 260

- Protein: 32g

- Total Fats: 10g

- Fiber: 1g

- Carbohydrates: 6g

Points: 3 Points

Honey Mustard Glazed Salmon

Time to Prepare: 10 minutes
Cooking Time: 12 minutes
Number of Servings: 4

Ingredients:

- 4 salmon fillets (about 4-6 ounces each)

- 3 tablespoons Dijon mustard

- 2 tablespoons honey

- 1 tablespoon olive oil

- 1 tablespoon lemon juice

- 2 cloves garlic, minced

- Salt and pepper, to taste

- Fresh parsley, chopped (for garnish)

Instructions List:

1. Preheat the oven to 400°F (200°C). Line a baking sheet with parchment paper or lightly grease it.

2. In a small bowl, whisk together Dijon mustard, honey, olive oil, lemon juice, minced garlic, salt, and pepper.

3. Place the salmon fillets on the prepared baking sheet.

4. Brush the honey mustard mixture evenly over the salmon fillets, coating them generously.

5. Bake in the preheated oven for 10-12 minutes, or until the salmon is cooked through and flakes easily with a fork.

6. Remove from the oven and let rest for a few minutes.

7. Garnish with chopped fresh parsley before serving.

Nutritional Information (per serving):

- Calories: 290

- Protein: 24g

- Total Fats: 14g

- Fiber: 0.5g

- Carbohydrates: 17g

Points: 4 Points

Lemon Dill Shrimp Skewers

Time to Prepare: 15 minutes
Cooking Time: 6 minutes
Number of Servings: 4

Ingredients:

- 1 pound large shrimp, peeled and deveined

- 2 tablespoons olive oil

- 2 tablespoons lemon juice

- 2 cloves garlic, minced

- 1 tablespoon fresh dill, chopped

- 1/2 teaspoon of salt

- 1/4 teaspoon of black pepper

- Lemon wedges (for serving)

Instructions List:

1. In a bowl, whisk together olive oil, lemon juice, minced garlic, chopped dill, salt, and black pepper.

2. Add the shrimp to the bowl and toss until evenly coated with the marinade. Let marinate for 10 minutes.

3. Preheat the grill or grill pan over medium-high heat.

4. Thread the marinated shrimp onto skewers, dividing them evenly.

5. Grill the shrimp skewers for about 2-3 minutes per side, or until they are pink and opaque.

6. Remove from the grill and serve immediately with lemon wedges on the side.

Nutritional Information (per serving):

- Calories: 156

- Protein: 24g

- Total Fats: 6g

- Fiber: 0.5g

- Carbohydrates: 2g

Points: 3 Points

Grilled Flank Steak with Chimichurri

Time to Prepare: 15 minutes
Cooking Time: 10 minutes
Number of Servings: 4

Ingredients:

- 1 lb flank steak
- Salt and pepper to taste
- 1 cup of fresh parsley, chopped
- 4 cloves garlic, minced
- 2 tablespoons fresh oregano leaves
- 1/4 cup of red wine vinegar
- 1/4 cup of olive oil
- 1/2 teaspoon of red pepper flakes

Instructions List:

1. Preheat the grill to medium-high heat.
2. Season the flank steak generously with salt and pepper on both sides.
3. In a blender or food processor, combine the parsley, garlic, oregano, red wine vinegar, olive oil, and red pepper flakes. Blend until smooth.
4. Grill the flank steak for about 4-5 minutes per side for medium-rare, or until desired doneness is reached.
5. Remove the steak from the grill and let it rest for 5 minutes.
6. Slice the steak thinly against the grain and serve with chimichurri sauce drizzled on top.

Nutritional Information (per serving):

- Calories: 306
- Protein: 24g
- Total Fats: 21g
- Fiber: 1g
- Carbohydrates: 3g

Points: 6 Points

Spicy Thai Beef Salad

Time to Prepare: 20 minutes
Cooking Time: 10 minutes
Number of Servings: 4

Ingredients:

- 1 lb flank steak

- Salt and pepper to taste

- 2 cups of mixed salad greens

- 1 cucumber, thinly sliced

- 1/2 red onion, thinly sliced

- 1/4 cup of fresh cilantro, chopped

- 1/4 cup of fresh mint leaves, chopped

- 2 tablespoons roasted peanuts, chopped

- 1 red chili, thinly sliced (optional)

Dressing:

- 3 tablespoons lime juice

- 2 tablespoons fish sauce

- 1 tablespoon soy sauce

- 1 tablespoon honey

- 1 tablespoon sesame oil

- 1 garlic clove, minced

- 1 teaspoon of fresh ginger, grated

Instructions List:

1. Season the flank steak with salt and pepper on both sides.

2. Heat a grill or grill pan over medium-high heat. Grill the steak for 4-5 minutes per side for medium-rare, or until desired doneness is reached. Remove from heat and let it rest for 5 minutes.

3. In a large bowl, combine the mixed salad greens, cucumber, red onion, cilantro, and mint leaves.

4. In a small bowl, whisk together the lime juice, fish sauce, soy sauce, honey, sesame oil, garlic, and ginger to make the dressing.

5. Thinly slice the grilled steak against the grain.

6. Add the sliced steak to the salad bowl, pour the dressing over the salad, and toss gently to combine.

7. Garnish with chopped peanuts and sliced red chili (if using) before serving.

Nutritional Information (per serving):

- Calories: 298

- Protein: 25g

- Total Fats: 13g

- Fiber: 3g

- Carbohydrates: 20g

Points: 5 Points

Chapter 7: Fish & Seafood

Lemon Herb Baked Cod

Time to Prepare: 10 minutes
Cooking Time: 15 minutes
Number of Servings: 4

Ingredients:

- 4 cod fillets (about 6 oz each)
- Salt and pepper to taste
- 2 tablespoons olive oil
- 2 cloves garlic, minced
- 1 tablespoon fresh parsley, chopped
- 1 tablespoon fresh dill, chopped
- 1 tablespoon fresh chives, chopped
- Zest of 1 lemon
- Juice of 1 lemon

Instructions List:

1. Preheat the oven to 400°F (200°C). Lightly grease a baking dish.
2. Season the cod fillets with salt and pepper on both sides, then place them in the prepared baking dish.
3. In a small bowl, combine the olive oil, minced garlic, chopped parsley, dill, chives, lemon zest, and lemon juice.
4. Spoon the herb mixture over the cod fillets, spreading it evenly.
5. Bake in the preheated oven for 12-15 minutes, or until the fish flakes easily with a fork.
6. Remove from the oven and serve hot.

Nutritional Information (per serving):

- Calories: 216
- Protein: 30g
- Total Fats: 8g
- Fiber: 0g
- Carbohydrates: 2g

Points: 3 Points

Shrimp Scampi Zoodles

Time to Prepare: 15 minutes
Cooking Time: 10 minutes
Number of Servings: 4

Ingredients:

- 1 lb large shrimp, peeled and deveined
- Salt and pepper to taste
- 4 medium zucchini, spiralized into noodles
- 2 tablespoons olive oil
- 4 cloves garlic, minced
- 1/4 teaspoon of red pepper flakes (optional)
- 1/4 cup of low-sodium chicken broth
- 2 tablespoons lemon juice
- 2 tablespoons chopped fresh parsley
- 1 tablespoon grated Parmesan cheese (optional)

Instructions List:

1. Season the shrimp with salt and pepper.

2. Heat 1 tablespoon of olive oil in a large skillet over medium heat. Add the shrimp and cook until pink and opaque, about 2-3 minutes per side. Remove the shrimp from the skillet and set aside.

3. In the same skillet, add the remaining tablespoon of olive oil. Add the minced garlic and red pepper flakes, if using, and cook until fragrant, about 1 minute.

4. Add the chicken broth and lemon juice to the skillet. Bring to a simmer and cook for 2 minutes.

5. Return the shrimp to the skillet and add the zucchini noodles. Toss everything together until the zucchini noodles are heated through and coated in the sauce, about 2-3 minutes.

6. Remove from heat and sprinkle with chopped parsley and grated Parmesan cheese, if desired, before serving.

Nutritional Information (per serving):

- Calories: 191
- Protein: 23g
- Total Fats: 9g
- Fiber: 2g
- Carbohydrates: 6g

Points: 4 Points

Grilled Salmon with Mango Salsa

Time to Prepare: 15 minutes
Cooking Time: 10 minutes
Number of Servings: 4

Ingredients:

- 4 salmon fillets (about 4-6 ounces each)

- Salt and pepper to taste

- 2 ripe mangoes, diced

- 1/2 red onion, finely chopped

- 1 jalapeño pepper, seeded and minced

- 1/4 cup of fresh cilantro, chopped

- 2 tablespoons lime juice

- 1 tablespoon olive oil

Instructions List:

1. Preheat the grill to medium-high heat.

2. Season the salmon fillets with salt and pepper.

3. In a bowl, combine the diced mangoes, red onion, jalapeño pepper, cilantro, lime juice, and olive oil to make the salsa. Season with salt and pepper to taste.

4. Grill the salmon fillets for 4-5 minutes per side, or until cooked through and flaky.

5. Remove the salmon from the grill and top each fillet with the mango salsa.

6. Serve immediately.

Nutritional Information (per serving):

- Calories: 320

- Protein: 34g

- Total Fats: 14g

- Fiber: 3g

- Carbohydrates: 16g

Points: 5 Points

Tuna Salad Lettuce Wraps

Time to Prepare: 10 minutes
Cooking Time: 0 minutes
Number of Servings: 4

Ingredients:

- 2 cans (5 ounces each) of tuna in water, drained

- 1/4 cup of plain Greek yogurt

- 2 tablespoons mayonnaise

- 1 celery stalk, finely chopped

- 1/4 red onion, finely chopped

- 1 tablespoon lemon juice

- Salt and pepper to taste

- 8 large lettuce leaves (such as Bibb or Romaine)

Instructions List:

1. In a bowl, combine the drained tuna, Greek yogurt, mayonnaise, celery, red onion, and lemon juice. Mix well.

2. Season the tuna salad with salt and pepper to taste.

3. Place a scoop of the tuna salad onto each lettuce leaf.

4. Wrap the lettuce around the tuna salad to form a lettuce wrap.

5. Serve immediately or refrigerate until ready to serve.

Nutritional Information (per serving):

- Calories: 140

- Protein: 18g

- Total Fats: 5g

- Fiber: 1g

- Carbohydrates: 4g

Points: 2 Points

Baked Lemon Herb Salmon

Time to Prepare: 10 minutes
Cooking Time: 15 minutes
Number of Servings: 4

Ingredients:

- 4 salmon fillets (4-6 ounces each)

- 2 tablespoons fresh lemon juice

- 2 cloves garlic, minced

- 2 tablespoons chopped fresh parsley

- 1 tablespoon chopped fresh dill

- Salt and pepper to taste

- Lemon slices for garnish

Instructions List:

1. Preheat the oven to 400°F (200°C). Line a baking sheet with parchment paper.

2. Place the salmon fillets on the prepared baking sheet.

3. In a small bowl, mix together the lemon juice, minced garlic, parsley, dill, salt, and pepper.

4. Spoon the lemon herb mixture evenly over the salmon fillets, spreading it to coat the tops.

5. Place a lemon slice on top of each salmon fillet for garnish.

6. Bake in the preheated oven for 12-15 minutes, or until the salmon is cooked through and flakes easily with a fork.

7. Remove from the oven and serve hot.

Nutritional Information (per serving):

- Calories: 250

- Protein: 34g

- Total Fats: 11g

- Fiber: 0g

- Carbohydrates: 2g

Points: 0 Points

Shrimp and Zucchini Noodles

Time to Prepare: 10 minutes
Cooking Time: 10 minutes
Number of Servings: 4

Ingredients:

- 1 lb medium shrimp, peeled and deveined

- 4 medium zucchinis, spiralized into noodles

- 2 cloves garlic, minced

- 1 tablespoon olive oil

- 1 teaspoon of paprika

- Salt and pepper to taste

- Fresh parsley for garnish

Instructions List:

1. Heat olive oil in a large skillet over medium heat. Add minced garlic and cook until fragrant, about 1 minute.

2. Add shrimp to the skillet and sprinkle with paprika, salt, and pepper. Cook until shrimp turn pink and opaque, about 2-3 minutes per side.

3. Add spiralized zucchini noodles to the skillet with the cooked shrimp. Cook, tossing gently, until the zucchini noodles are just tender, about 2-3 minutes.

4. Remove from heat and garnish with fresh parsley before serving.

Nutritional Information (per serving):

- Calories: 150

- Protein: 20g

- Total Fats: 5g

- Fiber: 3g

- Carbohydrates: 8g

Points: 0 Points

Coconut Curry Shrimp

Time to Prepare: 10 minutes
Cooking Time: 20 minutes
Number of Servings: 4

Ingredients:

- 1 lb medium shrimp, peeled and deveined

- 1 can (14 oz) coconut milk

- 1 onion, chopped

- 2 cloves garlic, minced

- 1 tablespoon ginger, grated

- 2 tablespoons curry powder

- 1 tablespoon olive oil

- Salt and pepper to taste

- Fresh cilantro for garnish

Instructions List:

1. Heat olive oil in a large skillet over medium heat. Add chopped onion and cook until softened, about 3-4 minutes.

2. Add minced garlic and grated ginger to the skillet. Cook for another 1-2 minutes until fragrant.

3. Stir in curry powder and cook for an additional minute.

4. Pour in the coconut milk and bring to a simmer.

5. Add the shrimp to the skillet and cook until pink and opaque, about 4-5 minutes.

6. Season with salt and pepper to taste.

7. Serve hot, garnished with fresh cilantro.

Nutritional Information (per serving):

- Calories: 270

- Protein: 20g

- Total Fats: 19g

- Fiber: 2g

- Carbohydrates: 7g

Points: 4 Points

Mediterranean Baked Sea Bass

Time to Prepare: 15 minutes
Cooking Time: 20 minutes
Number of Servings: 4

Ingredients:

- 4 sea bass fillets
- 2 tablespoons olive oil
- 4 cloves garlic, minced
- 1 tablespoon lemon juice
- 1 teaspoon of dried oregano
- 1 teaspoon of dried thyme
- 1 teaspoon of dried rosemary
- Salt and pepper to taste
- Lemon wedges for serving
- Fresh parsley for garnish

Instructions List:

1. Preheat the oven to 375°F (190°C). Lightly grease a baking dish.
2. Pat dry the sea bass fillets with paper towels and place them in the prepared baking dish.
3. In a small bowl, mix together olive oil, minced garlic, lemon juice, dried oregano, dried thyme, and dried rosemary.
4. Drizzle the olive oil mixture over the sea bass fillets, ensuring they are evenly coated.
5. Season the fillets with salt and pepper to taste.
6. Bake in the preheated oven for about 15-20 minutes, or until the fish is cooked through and flakes easily with a fork.
7. Remove from the oven and garnish with fresh parsley. Serve with lemon wedges on the side.

Nutritional Information (per serving):

- Calories: 240
- Protein: 28g
- Total Fats: 12g
- Fiber: 1g
- Carbohydrates: 2g

Points: 3 Points

Cajun Spiced Catfish

Time to Prepare: 10 minutes
Cooking Time: 15 minutes
Number of Servings: 4

Ingredients:

- 4 catfish fillets
- 2 tablespoons olive oil
- 2 teaspoons of paprika
- 1 teaspoon of garlic powder
- 1 teaspoon of onion powder
- 1 teaspoon of dried thyme
- 1 teaspoon of dried oregano
- 1/2 teaspoon of cayenne pepper
- Salt and pepper to taste
- Lemon wedges for serving
- Fresh parsley for garnish

Instructions List:

1. Preheat the oven to 375°F (190°C). Lightly grease a baking dish.

2. In a small bowl, mix together paprika, garlic powder, onion powder, dried thyme, dried oregano, cayenne pepper, salt, and pepper.

3. Pat dry the catfish fillets with paper towels and place them in the prepared baking dish.

4. Drizzle olive oil over the catfish fillets, then sprinkle the Cajun spice mixture evenly over each fillet, pressing gently to adhere.

5. Bake in the preheated oven for about 12-15 minutes, or until the catfish is cooked through and flakes easily with a fork.

6. Remove from the oven and let rest for a few minutes before serving.

7. Garnish with fresh parsley and serve with lemon wedges on the side.

Nutritional Information (per serving):

- Calories: 220
- Protein: 25g
- Total Fats: 12g
- Fiber: 1g
- Carbohydrates: 2g

Points: 4 Points

Sesame Ginger Glazed Mahi Mahi

Time to Prepare: 15 minutes
Cooking Time: 10 minutes
Number of Servings: 4

Ingredients:

- 4 mahi mahi fillets
- 3 tablespoons low-sodium soy sauce
- 2 tablespoons rice vinegar
- 2 tablespoons honey
- 1 tablespoon sesame oil
- 1 tablespoon grated ginger
- 2 cloves garlic, minced
- 1 teaspoon of cornstarch
- 1 tablespoon water
- Sesame seeds, for garnish
- Sliced green onions, for garnish

Instructions List:

1. In a small bowl, whisk together soy sauce, rice vinegar, honey, sesame oil, grated ginger, and minced garlic to make the glaze.

2. In a separate small bowl, mix cornstarch with water to make a slurry.

3. Heat a non-stick skillet over medium-high heat. Place the mahi mahi fillets in the skillet and cook for about 3-4 minutes on each side, or until cooked through and flaky.

4. Pour the glaze over the mahi mahi fillets in the skillet and let it simmer for 1-2 minutes, or until slightly thickened.

5. Brush the glaze over the fillets as they cook.

6. Once the mahi mahi is cooked and the glaze has thickened, remove from heat.

7. Serve the mahi mahi garnished with sesame seeds and sliced green onions.

Nutritional Information (per serving):

- Calories: 220
- Protein: 25g
- Total Fats: 6g
- Fiber: 0.5g
- Carbohydrates: 15g

Points: 5 Points

Smoked Salmon and Avocado Toast

Time to Prepare: 10 minutes
Cooking Time: 0 MINUTES
Number of Servings: 2

Ingredients:

- 4 slices whole grain bread, toasted
- 1 ripe avocado, mashed
- 100g smoked salmon
- 1 tablespoon chopped fresh dill
- 1 tablespoon lemon juice
- Salt and pepper, to taste
- Red pepper flakes, for garnish (optional)
- Lemon wedges, for serving

Instructions List:

1. In a small bowl, mix together the mashed avocado, chopped dill, lemon juice, salt, and pepper.
2. Spread the avocado mixture evenly on each slice of toasted bread.
3. Top each toast with smoked salmon, dividing it equally between the slices.
4. Garnish with red pepper flakes, if desired.
5. Serve with lemon wedges on the side.

Nutritional Information (per serving):

- Calories: 260
- Protein: 15g
- Total Fats: 13g
- Fiber: 6g
- Carbohydrates: 22g

Points: 4 Points

Greek-Style Grilled Octopus

Time to Prepare: 15 minutes
Cooking Time: 45 minutes
Number of Servings: 4

Ingredients:

- 2 lbs octopus, cleaned and tentacles separated
- 2 tablespoons olive oil
- 2 cloves garlic, minced

- 2 tablespoons fresh lemon juice

- 1 teaspoon of dried oregano

- Salt and pepper, to taste

- Lemon wedges, for serving

- Chopped fresh parsley, for garnish

Instructions List:

1. Preheat grill to medium-high heat.

2. In a large bowl, combine the olive oil, minced garlic, lemon juice, dried oregano, salt, and pepper.

3. Add the cleaned octopus to the bowl and toss to coat evenly with the marinade.

4. Place the octopus tentacles on the grill and cook for about 3-4 minutes per side, or until charred and cooked through.

5. Remove the octopus from the grill and transfer to a serving platter.

6. Garnish with chopped parsley and serve with lemon wedges on the side.

Nutritional Information (per serving):

- Calories: 180

- Protein: 25g

- Total Fats: 7g

- Fiber: 0g

- Carbohydrates: 2g

Points: 3 Points

Chapter 8: Vegetarian

Roasted Vegetable Quinoa Bowl

Time to Prepare: 15 minutes
Cooking Time: 25 minutes
Number of Servings: 4

Ingredients:

- 1 cup of quinoa, rinsed
- 2 cups of vegetable broth
- 1 large sweet potato, peeled and diced
- 2 cups of broccoli florets
- 1 red bell pepper, sliced
- 1 yellow bell pepper, sliced
- 1 small red onion, sliced
- 2 tablespoons olive oil
- 1 teaspoon of garlic powder
- 1 teaspoon of paprika
- Salt and pepper, to taste
- 2 tablespoons balsamic vinegar
- Fresh parsley, for garnish

Instructions List:

1. Preheat oven to 400°F (200°C).

2. In a saucepan, combine the quinoa and vegetable broth. Bring to a boil, then reduce heat to low, cover, and simmer for 15-20 minutes, or until quinoa is cooked and liquid is absorbed.

3. While the quinoa is cooking, spread the diced sweet potato, broccoli florets, sliced bell peppers, and red onion on a large baking sheet.

4. Drizzle the olive oil over the vegetables and sprinkle with garlic powder, paprika, salt, and pepper. Toss to coat evenly.

5. Roast the vegetables in the preheated oven for 20-25 minutes, or until tender and slightly browned, stirring halfway through.

6. Once the quinoa and vegetables are cooked, assemble the bowls by dividing the quinoa and roasted vegetables among serving bowls.

7. Drizzle each bowl with balsamic vinegar and garnish with fresh parsley.

Nutritional Information (per serving):

- Calories: 320
- Protein: 8g

- Total Fats: 8g

- Fiber: 9g

- Carbohydrates: 55g

Points: 6 Points

Stuffed Bell Peppers with Quinoa and Black Beans

Time to Prepare: 20 minutes
Cooking Time: 40 minutes
Number of Servings: 4

Ingredients:

- 4 large bell peppers, tops cut off and seeds removed

- 1 cup of quinoa, rinsed

- 2 cups of vegetable broth

- 1 can (15 oz) black beans, drained and rinsed

- 1 cup of corn kernels (fresh or frozen)

- 1 cup of diced tomatoes

- 1 small red onion, diced

- 1 teaspoon of cumin

- 1 teaspoon of chili powder

- 1/2 teaspoon of garlic powder

- Salt and pepper, to taste

- 1/2 cup of shredded low-fat cheddar cheese

- Fresh cilantro, for garnish

Instructions List:

1. Preheat oven to 375°F (190°C).

2. In a saucepan, combine the quinoa and vegetable broth. Bring to a boil, then reduce heat to low, cover, and simmer for 15-20 minutes, or until quinoa is cooked and liquid is absorbed.

3. In a large bowl, mix the cooked quinoa, black beans, corn, diced tomatoes, red onion, cumin, chili powder, garlic powder, salt, and pepper.

4. Stuff each bell pepper with the quinoa mixture, pressing down to pack it tightly.

5. Place the stuffed peppers in a baking dish and cover with foil.

6. Bake in the preheated oven for 30 minutes. Remove the foil, sprinkle the tops with shredded cheddar cheese, and bake for an additional 10 minutes, or until the cheese is melted and the peppers are tender.

7. Garnish with fresh cilantro before serving.

Nutritional Information (per serving):

- Calories: 290

- Protein: 12g

- Total Fats: 6g

- Fiber: 10g

- Carbohydrates: 48g

Points: 5 Points

Cauliflower Rice Stir-Fry

Time to Prepare: 15 minutes
Cooking Time: 15 minutes
Number of Servings: 4

Ingredients:

- 1 large head cauliflower, grated or processed into rice-sized pieces

- 1 tablespoon olive oil

- 1 small onion, diced

- 2 cloves garlic, minced

- 1 cup of frozen peas and carrots, thawed

- 1 red bell pepper, diced

- 3 green onions, sliced

- 3 tablespoons low-sodium soy sauce

- 1 tablespoon sesame oil

- 1/2 teaspoon of ground ginger

- 1/4 teaspoon of black pepper

- 2 large eggs, lightly beaten

- Fresh cilantro, for garnish

Instructions List:

1. Heat olive oil in a large skillet or wok over medium heat. Add the diced onion and cook until softened, about 3 minutes.

2. Add the minced garlic and cook for an additional 1 minute.

3. Stir in the grated cauliflower, peas and carrots, red bell pepper, and green onions. Cook for about 5-7 minutes, or until the vegetables are tender.

4. In a small bowl, mix the soy sauce, sesame oil, ground ginger, and black pepper. Pour over the vegetable mixture, stirring to combine.

5. Push the vegetables to one side of the skillet and pour the beaten eggs into the other side. Scramble the eggs until fully cooked, then mix them into the vegetable mixture.

6. Serve the stir-fry hot, garnished with fresh cilantro.

Nutritional Information (per serving):

- Calories: 140

- Protein: 6g

- Total Fats: 7g

- Fiber: 5g

- Carbohydrates: 15g

Points: 4 Points

Eggplant Parmesan

Time to Prepare: 20 minutes
Cooking Time: 40 minutes
Number of Servings: 6

Ingredients:

- 2 large eggplants, sliced into 1/4-inch rounds

- 1 teaspoon of salt

- 1 cup of whole wheat breadcrumbs

- 1/2 cup of grated Parmesan cheese

- 1 teaspoon of dried oregano

- 1 teaspoon of dried basil

- 1/2 teaspoon of garlic powder

- 2 large eggs, beaten

- 2 cups of marinara sauce (no sugar added)

- 1 1/2 cups of shredded part-skim mozzarella cheese

- Cooking spray

Instructions List:

1. Preheat oven to 375°F (190°C). Lightly grease a large baking sheet with cooking spray.

2. Arrange the eggplant slices in a single layer on paper towels and sprinkle both sides with salt. Let them sit for 20 minutes to draw out moisture. Pat dry with paper towels.

3. In a shallow dish, mix together breadcrumbs, Parmesan cheese, oregano, basil, and garlic powder.

4. Dip each eggplant slice in the beaten eggs, then coat with the breadcrumb mixture, pressing gently to adhere. Place the coated slices on the prepared baking sheet.

5. Bake the eggplant slices for 20 minutes, flipping halfway through, until they are golden brown and crisp.

6. In a 9x13-inch baking dish, spread a thin layer of marinara sauce. Arrange a layer of baked eggplant slices over the sauce. Top with more marinara sauce and a sprinkle of mozzarella cheese. Repeat the layers, ending with a layer of marinara sauce and mozzarella cheese on top.

7. Bake the assembled dish for 20 minutes, or until the cheese is melted and bubbly. Let it cool for a few minutes before serving.

Nutritional Information (per serving):

- Calories: 260

- Protein: 15g

- Total Fats: 10g

- Fiber: 7g

- Carbohydrates: 27g

Points: 7 Points

Greek Salad with Tzatziki Dressing

Time to Prepare: 15 minutes
Cooking Time: 0 minutes
Number of Servings: 4

Ingredients:

- 4 cups chopped romaine lettuce

- 1 cup of cherry tomatoes, halved

- 1 cucumber, diced

- 1/2 red onion, thinly sliced

- 1/2 cup of kalamata olives, pitted and sliced

- 1/2 cup of fat-free feta cheese, crumbled

Tzatziki Dressing:

- 1 cup of non-fat Greek yogurt

- 1 tablespoon lemon juice

- 1 tablespoon fresh dill, chopped

- 1 garlic clove, minced

- 1/2 cucumber, grated and excess water squeezed out

- Salt and pepper to taste

Instructions List:

1. In a large bowl, combine romaine lettuce, cherry tomatoes, cucumber, red onion, kalamata olives, and feta cheese.

2. In a separate bowl, mix together the Greek yogurt, lemon juice, fresh dill, minced garlic, and grated cucumber. Season with salt and pepper to taste.

3. Pour the Tzatziki dressing over the salad and toss gently to combine.

4. Serve immediately or chill until ready to serve.

Nutritional Information (per serving):

- Calories: 110

- Protein: 8g

- Total Fats: 3g

- Fiber: 3g

- Carbohydrates: 10g

Points: 0 Points

Cauliflower Fried Rice

Time to Prepare: 10 minutes
Cooking Time: 15 minutes
Number of Servings: 4

Ingredients:

- 1 medium head of cauliflower, grated or pulsed into rice-sized pieces

- 1 tablespoon olive oil

- 1 small onion, diced

- 2 garlic cloves, minced

- 1 cup of frozen peas and carrots, thawed

- 2 eggs, lightly beaten

- 3 tablespoons low-sodium soy sauce

- 1 teaspoon of sesame oil

- 2 green onions, sliced

- Salt and pepper to taste

Instructions List:

1. Heat olive oil in a large skillet over medium heat. Add diced onion and cook until softened, about 3-4 minutes.

2. Add minced garlic and cook for another minute.

3. Stir in the cauliflower rice, peas, and carrots. Cook, stirring frequently, until the vegetables are tender, about 5-7 minutes.

4. Push the vegetables to one side of the skillet and pour the beaten eggs into the other side. Scramble the eggs until cooked through, then mix with the vegetables.

5. Stir in the soy sauce and sesame oil until well mixed. Season with salt and pepper to taste.

6. Remove from heat and garnish with sliced green onions before serving.

Nutritional Information (per serving):

- Calories: 120

- Protein: 6g

- Total Fats: 5g

- Fiber: 4g

- Carbohydrates: 10g

Points: 0 Points

Zucchini Noodles with Pesto

Time to Prepare: 10 minutes
Cooking Time: 5 minutes
Number of Servings: 4

Ingredients:

- 4 medium zucchinis, spiralized into noodles

- 1 cup of fresh basil leaves

- 2 cloves garlic

- 2 tablespoons nutritional yeast

- 2 tablespoons pine nuts

- 1/4 cup of vegetable broth

- Salt and pepper to taste

- 1 teaspoon of olive oil

Instructions List:

1. Place the basil leaves, garlic, nutritional yeast, pine nuts, and vegetable broth in a food processor. Blend until smooth. Season with salt and pepper to taste.

2. Heat the olive oil in a large skillet over medium heat. Add the zucchini noodles and cook, tossing gently, for about 3-4 minutes until they are just tender.

3. Remove from heat and toss the zucchini noodles with the prepared pesto until evenly coated.

4. Serve immediately.

Nutritional Information (per serving):

- Calories: 75

- Protein: 4g

- Total Fats: 3g

- Fiber: 3g

- Carbohydrates: 9g

Points: 0 Points

Portobello Mushroom Burger

Time to Prepare: 10 minutes
Cooking Time: 15 minutes
Number of Servings: 4

Ingredients:

- 4 large Portobello mushroom caps, stems removed
- 2 tablespoons balsamic vinegar
- 1 tablespoon olive oil
- 1 tablespoon low-sodium soy sauce
- 1 teaspoon of garlic powder
- 4 whole wheat burger buns
- 4 slices tomato
- 4 lettuce leaves
- 1 small red onion, thinly sliced
- Salt and pepper to taste

Instructions List:

1. Preheat the grill to medium-high heat.
2. In a small bowl, whisk together the balsamic vinegar, olive oil, soy sauce, and garlic powder.
3. Brush the mushroom caps with the balsamic mixture, making sure to coat both sides. Season with salt and pepper to taste.
4. Place the mushrooms on the grill and cook for about 5-7 minutes on each side, until tender and slightly charred.
5. Toast the whole wheat burger buns on the grill for about 1-2 minutes, until lightly browned.
6. Assemble the burgers by placing a grilled Portobello mushroom cap on each bun bottom. Top with a slice of tomato, a lettuce leaf, and red onion slices. Cover with the bun tops.
7. Serve immediately.

Nutritional Information (per serving):

- Calories: 180
- Protein: 5g
- Total Fats: 5g
- Fiber: 4g
- Carbohydrates: 28g

Points: 3 Points

Ratatouille

Time to Prepare: 15 minutes
Cooking Time: 45 minutes
Number of Servings: 6

Ingredients:

- 1 large eggplant, diced
- 1 zucchini, sliced
- 1 yellow squash, sliced
- 1 red bell pepper, chopped
- 1 yellow bell pepper, chopped
- 1 onion, chopped
- 3 cloves garlic, minced
- 4 large tomatoes, chopped
- 2 tablespoons olive oil
- 1 teaspoon of dried thyme
- 1 teaspoon of dried basil
- 1 teaspoon of dried oregano
- Salt and pepper to taste
- Fresh basil leaves for garnish

Instructions List:

1. Preheat the oven to 375°F (190°C).
2. In a large skillet, heat the olive oil over medium heat. Add the onion and garlic, and sauté until soft.
3. Add the eggplant, zucchini, yellow squash, and bell peppers to the skillet. Cook for about 10 minutes, stirring occasionally, until the vegetables begin to soften.
4. Add the tomatoes, thyme, basil, oregano, salt, and pepper to the skillet. Stir to combine.
5. Transfer the mixture to a large baking dish. Bake in the preheated oven for 30 minutes, until the vegetables are tender.
6. Garnish with fresh basil leaves before serving.

Nutritional Information (per serving):

- Calories: 110
- Protein: 2g
- Total Fats: 5g
- Fiber: 4g
- Carbohydrates: 14g

Points: 2 Points

Spinach and Ricotta Stuffed Shells

Time to Prepare: 20 minutes
Cooking Time: 40 minutes
Number of Servings: 6

Ingredients:

- 18 jumbo pasta shells
- 2 cups of ricotta cheese
- 1 cup of shredded mozzarella cheese, divided
- 1/2 cup of grated Parmesan cheese
- 1 large egg, beaten
- 1 teaspoon of dried basil
- 1 teaspoon of dried oregano
- 1/2 teaspoon of garlic powder
- 10 ounces frozen chopped spinach, thawed and drained
- 2 cups of marinara sauce
- Salt and pepper to taste

Instructions List:

1. Preheat the oven to 375°F (190°C).
2. Cook the jumbo pasta shells according to package directions. Drain and set aside.
3. In a large bowl, mix together the ricotta cheese, 1/2 cup of mozzarella cheese, Parmesan cheese, beaten egg, basil, oregano, garlic powder, spinach, salt, and pepper.
4. Spread 1 cup of marinara sauce on the bottom of a 9x13 inch baking dish.
5. Stuff each pasta shell with the spinach and ricotta mixture and place in the baking dish.
6. Pour the remaining marinara sauce over the stuffed shells and sprinkle with the remaining 1/2 cup of mozzarella cheese.
7. Cover the baking dish with aluminum foil and bake for 30 minutes. Remove the foil and bake for an additional 10 minutes, until the cheese is melted and bubbly.

Nutritional Information (per serving):

- Calories: 280
- Protein: 16g
- Total Fats: 12g
- Fiber: 3g
- Carbohydrates: 27g

Points: 6 Points

Sweet Potato and Black Bean Enchiladas

Time to Prepare: 20 minutes
Cooking Time: 40 minutes
Number of Servings: 6

Ingredients:

- 2 large sweet potatoes, peeled and diced

- 1 can (15 oz) black beans, drained and rinsed

- 1 cup of corn kernels (fresh, frozen, or canned)

- 1 small red onion, diced

- 2 cloves garlic, minced

- 1 teaspoon of ground cumin

- 1 teaspoon of chili powder

- 1/2 teaspoon of smoked paprika

- Salt and pepper to taste

- 8 whole wheat tortillas

- 2 cups of enchilada sauce

- 1 cup of shredded reduced-fat cheddar cheese

- Fresh cilantro, chopped (optional, for garnish)

Instructions List:

1. Preheat the oven to 375°F (190°C).

2. In a large skillet, cook the sweet potatoes over medium heat until tender, about 10 minutes. Add a small amount of water if needed to prevent sticking.

3. Add the black beans, corn, red onion, garlic, cumin, chili powder, smoked paprika, salt, and pepper to the skillet. Cook for an additional 5 minutes until the vegetables are well mixed and heated through.

4. Spread 1/2 cup of enchilada sauce on the bottom of a 9x13 inch baking dish.

5. Place a tortilla on a flat surface and spoon about 1/2 cup of the sweet potato and black bean mixture onto the center. Roll up the tortilla and place seam-side down in the baking dish. Repeat with the remaining tortillas and filling.

6. Pour the remaining enchilada sauce over the top of the rolled tortillas and sprinkle with the shredded cheese.

7. Cover the dish with aluminum foil and bake for 20 minutes. Remove the foil and bake for an additional 10 minutes, or until the cheese is melted and bubbly.

8. Garnish with fresh cilantro if desired before serving.

Nutritional Information (per serving):

- Calories: 320

- Protein: 12g

- Total Fats: 9g

- Fiber: 9g

- Carbohydrates: 50g

Points: 5 Points

Caprese Stuffed Portobellos

Time to Prepare: 15 minutes
Cooking Time: 20 minutes
Number of Servings: 4

Ingredients:

- 4 large portobello mushrooms

- 2 medium tomatoes, sliced

- 4 ounces fresh mozzarella cheese, sliced

- 1/4 cup of fresh basil leaves, chopped

- 2 cloves garlic, minced

- 2 tablespoons balsamic vinegar

- 2 teaspoons of olive oil

- Salt and pepper to taste

Instructions List:

1. Preheat the oven to 400°F (200°C). Line a baking sheet with parchment paper.

2. Remove the stems from the portobello mushrooms and gently scrape out the gills using a spoon.

3. In a small bowl, whisk together the minced garlic, balsamic vinegar, olive oil, salt, and pepper.

4. Brush both sides of the portobello mushrooms with the balsamic mixture and place them gill-side up on the prepared baking sheet.

5. Divide the sliced tomatoes, mozzarella cheese, and chopped basil evenly among the mushrooms, layering them inside each mushroom cap.

6. Bake in the preheated oven for 15-20 minutes, or until the mushrooms are tender and the cheese is melted and bubbly.

7. Serve hot, garnished with additional fresh basil if desired.

Nutritional Information (per serving):

- Calories: 140

- Protein: 9g

- Total Fats: 8g

- Fiber: 2g

- Carbohydrates: 10g

Points: 3 Points

Lentil Shepherd's Pie

Time to Prepare: 20 minutes
Cooking Time: 45 minutes
Number of Servings: 6

Ingredients:

- 1 cup of dry green lentils

- 3 cups vegetable broth

- 2 tablespoons olive oil

- 1 onion, diced

- 2 carrots, diced

- 2 stalks celery, diced

- 2 cloves garlic, minced

- 1 teaspoon of dried thyme

- 1 teaspoon of dried rosemary

- Salt and pepper to taste

- 1 cup of frozen peas

- 4 cups mashed potatoes (prepared)

Instructions List:

1. Preheat the oven to 375°F (190°C).

2. In a medium saucepan, combine the dry lentils and vegetable broth. Bring to a boil over medium-high heat, then reduce the heat to low and simmer for 20-25 minutes, or until the lentils are tender and the broth is absorbed.

3. While the lentils are cooking, heat the olive oil in a large skillet over medium heat. Add the diced onion, carrots, and celery, and sauté for 5-7 minutes, or until the vegetables are softened.

4. Add the minced garlic, dried thyme, and dried rosemary to the skillet, and cook for an additional 1-2 minutes, until fragrant.

5. Once the lentils are cooked, add them to the skillet with the cooked vegetables. Stir in the frozen peas and season with salt and pepper to taste. Cook for another 2-3 minutes to heat the peas through.

6. Transfer the lentil mixture to a 9x13-inch baking dish. Spread the mashed potatoes evenly over the top.

7. Place the baking dish in the preheated oven and bake for 20-25 minutes, or until the mashed potatoes are lightly golden on top.

8. Serve hot.

Nutritional Information (per serving):

- Calories: 320
- Protein: 12g
- Total Fats: 6g
- Fiber: 12g
- Carbohydrates: 55g

Points: 4 Points

Chapter 9: Soups & Stews

Minestrone Soup

Time to Prepare: 15 minutes
Cooking Time: 30 minutes
Number of Servings: 6

Ingredients:

- 1 tablespoon olive oil

- 1 onion, diced

- 2 carrots, diced

- 2 celery stalks, diced

- 3 cloves garlic, minced

- 1 zucchini, diced

- 1 yellow squash, diced

- 1 can (14 oz) diced tomatoes

- 6 cups vegetable broth

- 1 can (15 oz) kidney beans, drained and rinsed

- 1 cup of small pasta (such as ditalini or macaroni)

- 1 teaspoon of dried basil

- 1 teaspoon of dried oregano

- Salt and pepper to taste

- 2 cups of chopped spinach or kale

- Grated Parmesan cheese, for serving (optional)

Instructions List:

1. In a large pot, heat the olive oil over medium heat. Add the diced onion, carrots, and celery. Cook, stirring occasionally, until the vegetables are softened, about 5-7 minutes.

2. Add the minced garlic, diced zucchini, and yellow squash to the pot. Cook for another 3-4 minutes.

3. Stir in the diced tomatoes (with their juices), vegetable broth, kidney beans, dried basil, dried oregano, salt, and pepper. Bring the soup to a boil, then reduce the heat to low and let it simmer for 15-20 minutes.

4. Meanwhile, cook the pasta according to the package instructions until al dente. Drain and set aside.

5. Once the soup has simmered and the vegetables are tender, add the chopped spinach or kale to the pot. Stir until the greens are wilted.

6. Add the cooked pasta to the soup and stir to combine. Taste and adjust the seasoning if needed.

7. Serve hot, garnished with grated Parmesan cheese if desired.

Nutritional Information (per serving):

- Calories: 240

- Protein: 9g

- Total Fats: 3g

- Fiber: 8g

- Carbohydrates: 45g

Points: 3 Points

Thai Coconut Curry Soup

Time to Prepare: 15 minutes
Cooking Time: 25 minutes
Number of Servings: 4

Ingredients:

- 1 tablespoon coconut oil

- 1 onion, diced

- 2 cloves garlic, minced

- 1 tablespoon grated ginger

- 2 tablespoons Thai red curry paste

- 4 cups vegetable broth

- 1 can (14 oz) coconut milk

- 2 cups of diced sweet potatoes

- 1 cup of sliced mushrooms

- 1 red bell pepper, sliced

- 1 cup of diced tofu or cooked chicken (optional)

- 2 tablespoons soy sauce

- 1 tablespoon brown sugar

- Juice of 1 lime

- Salt and pepper to taste

- Fresh cilantro, for garnish

- Cooked rice or noodles, for serving (optional)

Instructions List:

1. In a large pot, heat the coconut oil over medium heat. Add the diced onion and cook until softened, about 3-4 minutes.

2. Add the minced garlic, grated ginger, and Thai red curry paste to the pot. Cook for another 2 minutes, stirring constantly.

3. Pour in the vegetable broth and coconut milk, stirring to combine.

4. Add the diced sweet potatoes to the pot and bring the soup to a simmer. Let it cook for 10 minutes.

5. After 10 minutes, add the sliced mushrooms, red bell pepper, and diced tofu or chicken (if using) to the pot. Cook for an additional 10-15 minutes, or until the sweet potatoes are tender.

6. Stir in the soy sauce, brown sugar, and lime juice. Taste and adjust the seasoning with salt and pepper as needed.

7. Serve hot, garnished with fresh cilantro. Serve over cooked rice or noodles if desired.

Nutritional Information (per serving):

- Calories: 340
- Protein: 8g
- Total Fats: 24g
- Fiber: 6g
- Carbohydrates: 28g

Points: 5 Points

White Bean and Kale Soup

Time to Prepare: 10 minutes
Cooking Time: 30 minutes
Number of Servings: 6

Ingredients:

- 1 tablespoon olive oil
- 1 onion, diced
- 2 cloves garlic, minced
- 2 carrots, diced
- 2 celery stalks, diced
- 4 cups vegetable broth
- 2 cans (15 oz each) white beans, drained and rinsed
- 1 can (14 oz) diced tomatoes
- 1 teaspoon of dried thyme
- 1 teaspoon of dried rosemary
- Salt and pepper to taste
- 4 cups chopped kale

Instructions List:

1. Heat the olive oil in a large pot over medium heat. Add the diced onion and cook until translucent, about 3-4 minutes.

2. Add the minced garlic, diced carrots, and diced celery to the pot. Cook for another 3-4 minutes, stirring occasionally.

3. Pour in the vegetable broth, white beans, diced tomatoes, dried thyme, and dried rosemary. Season with salt and pepper to taste.

4. Bring the soup to a simmer and let it cook for 20 minutes, stirring occasionally.

5. Add the chopped kale to the pot and cook for an additional 5-7 minutes, or until the kale is wilted and tender.

6. Taste and adjust the seasoning if needed.

7. Serve hot.

Nutritional Information (per serving):

- Calories: 210

- Protein: 9g

- Total Fats: 3g

- Fiber: 9g

- Carbohydrates: 38g

Points: 2 Points

Butternut Squash Bisque

Time to Prepare: 15 minutes
Cooking Time: 40 minutes
Number of Servings: 6

Ingredients:

- 1 tablespoon olive oil

- 1 onion, chopped

- 2 cloves garlic, minced

- 1 butternut squash, peeled, seeded, and cubed

- 2 carrots, chopped

- 2 celery stalks, chopped

- 4 cups vegetable broth

- 1 teaspoon of dried thyme

- 1/2 teaspoon of ground nutmeg

- Salt and pepper to taste

- 1/2 cup of unsweetened almond milk

- 2 tablespoons chopped fresh parsley (for garnish, optional)

Instructions List:

1. In a large pot, heat the olive oil over medium heat. Add the chopped onion and cook until softened, about 5 minutes.

2. Add the minced garlic and cook for another minute until fragrant.

3. Add the cubed butternut squash, chopped carrots, and chopped celery to the pot. Stir to combine with the onions and garlic.

4. Pour in the vegetable broth and add the dried thyme, ground nutmeg, salt, and pepper.

5. Bring the mixture to a boil, then reduce the heat to low and simmer for about 30 minutes, or until the vegetables are tender.

6. Using an immersion blender, puree the soup until smooth. Alternatively, you can carefully transfer the soup to a blender and puree in batches.

7. Stir in the unsweetened almond milk until well mixed.

8. Taste the soup and adjust the seasoning if needed.

9. Serve hot, garnished with chopped fresh parsley if desired.

Nutritional Information (per serving):

- Calories: 130

- Protein: 2g

- Total Fats: 4g

- Fiber: 5g

- Carbohydrates: 24g

Points: 4 Points

Vegetable Lentil Soup

Time to Prepare: 15 minutes
Cooking Time: 40 minutes
Number of Servings: 6

Ingredients:

- 1 tablespoon olive oil

- 1 onion, diced

- 2 carrots, diced

- 2 celery stalks, diced

- 2 cloves garlic, minced

- 1 cup of dry green lentils, rinsed

- 1 can (14 oz) diced tomatoes

- 6 cups vegetable broth

- 1 teaspoon of dried thyme

- 1 teaspoon of dried oregano

- Salt and pepper to taste

- 2 cups of chopped spinach or kale

- Fresh parsley, chopped (for garnish, optional)

Instructions List:

1. In a large pot, heat the olive oil over medium heat. Add the diced onion, carrots, and celery. Cook until the vegetables are softened, about 5-7 minutes.

2. Add the minced garlic and cook for an additional minute until fragrant.

3. Stir in the rinsed lentils, diced tomatoes, vegetable broth, dried thyme, dried oregano, salt, and pepper.

4. Bring the soup to a boil, then reduce the heat to low. Cover and simmer for about 30 minutes, or until the lentils are tender.

5. Stir in the chopped spinach or kale and cook for another 5 minutes until wilted.

6. Taste the soup and adjust the seasoning if needed.

7. Serve hot, garnished with fresh parsley if desired.

Nutritional Information (per serving):

- Calories: 210

- Protein: 11g

- Total Fats: 3g

- Fiber: 9g

- Carbohydrates: 36g

Points: 0 Points

Mexican Chicken and Corn Soup

Time to Prepare: 10 minutes
Cooking Time: 25 minutes
Number of Servings: 4

Ingredients:

- 1 tablespoon olive oil

- 1 onion, diced

- 2 cloves garlic, minced

- 1 bell pepper, diced

- 1 jalapeño pepper, seeded and diced

- 1 teaspoon of ground cumin

- 1 teaspoon of chili powder

- 1 can (14 oz) diced tomatoes

- 4 cups low-sodium chicken broth

- 2 cups of shredded cooked chicken breast

- 1 cup of corn kernels (fresh or frozen)
- Salt and pepper to taste
- Fresh cilantro, chopped (for garnish, optional)
- Lime wedges (for serving, optional)
- Avocado slices (for serving, optional)

Instructions List:

1. Heat the olive oil in a large pot over medium heat. Add the diced onion and cook until softened, about 3-4 minutes.
2. Add the minced garlic, diced bell pepper, and diced jalapeño pepper. Cook for another 2-3 minutes until fragrant.
3. Stir in the ground cumin and chili powder, and cook for 1 minute.
4. Add the diced tomatoes (with their juices), chicken broth, shredded chicken breast, and corn kernels to the pot. Season with salt and pepper to taste.
5. Bring the soup to a simmer and cook for 15-20 minutes, allowing the flavors to meld together.
6. Taste and adjust seasoning if necessary.
7. Serve hot, garnished with chopped cilantro and lime wedges if desired. Add avocado slices on top if desired.

Nutritional Information (per serving):

- Calories: 250
- Protein: 22g
- Total Fats: 8g
- Fiber: 5g
- Carbohydrates: 24g

Points: 0 Points

Cabbage Soup

Time to Prepare: 15 minutes
Cooking Time: 25 minutes
Number of Servings: 6

Ingredients:

- 1 tablespoon olive oil
- 1 onion, chopped
- 2 cloves garlic, minced
- 4 cups low-sodium vegetable broth
- 1 head cabbage, chopped
- 2 carrots, diced

MY COMPLETE PROGRAM NEW COOKBOOK 2024

- 2 stalks celery, diced

- 1 can (14 oz) diced tomatoes

- 1 teaspoon of dried thyme

- Salt and pepper to taste

- Fresh parsley, chopped (for garnish, optional)

Instructions List:

1. In a large pot, heat the olive oil over medium heat. Add the chopped onion and cook until softened, about 3-4 minutes.

2. Add the minced garlic and cook for an additional 1 minute until fragrant.

3. Pour in the vegetable broth and bring to a simmer.

4. Add the chopped cabbage, diced carrots, diced celery, diced tomatoes (with their juices), and dried thyme to the pot. Season with salt and pepper to taste.

5. Simmer the soup for 20-25 minutes until the vegetables are tender.

6. Taste and adjust seasoning if necessary.

7. Serve hot, garnished with chopped fresh parsley if desired.

Nutritional Information (per serving):

- Calories: 90

- Protein: 3g

- Total Fats: 3g

- Fiber: 5g

- Carbohydrates: 15g

Points: 0 Points

Chicken Tortilla Soup

Time to Prepare: 15 minutes
Cooking Time: 25 minutes
Number of Servings: 6

Ingredients:

- 1 tablespoon olive oil

- 1 onion, chopped

- 2 cloves garlic, minced

- 1 bell pepper, diced

- 1 jalapeño pepper, seeded and minced

- 1 can (14 oz) diced tomatoes

- 1 can (4 oz) diced green chilies

- 4 cups low-sodium chicken broth

- 1 teaspoon of chili powder

- 1 teaspoon of cumin

- Salt and pepper to taste

- 2 cups of cooked shredded chicken breast

- 1 cup of frozen corn kernels

- 1 lime, juiced

- 1/4 cup of fresh cilantro, chopped

- 4 corn tortillas, cut into strips

- Cooking spray

Instructions List:

1. Heat olive oil in a large pot over medium heat. Add onion, garlic, bell pepper, and jalapeño pepper. Cook until vegetables are softened, about 5 minutes.

2. Add diced tomatoes, green chilies, chicken broth, chili powder, cumin, salt, and pepper. Bring to a simmer and cook for 10 minutes.

3. Stir in shredded chicken, corn, lime juice, and chopped cilantro. Simmer for an additional 10 minutes.

4. Meanwhile, preheat the oven to 375°F (190°C). Spread the tortilla strips on a baking sheet, spray with cooking spray, and bake until golden and crisp, about 10 minutes.

5. Serve the soup hot, topped with baked tortilla strips.

Nutritional Information (per serving):

- Calories: 240

- Protein: 18g

- Total Fats: 6g

- Fiber: 5g

- Carbohydrates: 29g

Points: 4 Points

Lentil and Vegetable Stew

Time to Prepare: 15 minutes
Cooking Time: 30 minutes
Number of Servings: 4

Ingredients:

- 1 tablespoon olive oil

- 1 onion, diced

- 2 carrots, diced

- 2 celery stalks, diced

- 2 cloves garlic, minced

- 1 cup of dried green lentils, rinsed

- 4 cups vegetable broth

- 1 can (14 oz) diced tomatoes

- 1 teaspoon of dried thyme

- 1 teaspoon of dried oregano

- Salt and pepper to taste

- 2 cups of chopped spinach or kale

- 1 tablespoon balsamic vinegar

- Fresh parsley for garnish (optional)

Instructions List:

1. In a large pot, heat olive oil over medium heat. Add onion, carrots, and celery. Cook until vegetables are softened, about 5 minutes.

2. Add minced garlic and cook for another minute.

3. Stir in the rinsed lentils, vegetable broth, diced tomatoes, thyme, oregano, salt, and pepper. Bring to a boil.

4. Reduce heat to low, cover, and simmer for about 20-25 minutes or until lentils are tender.

5. Stir in chopped spinach or kale and balsamic vinegar. Cook for an additional 5 minutes.

6. Adjust seasoning if needed. Serve hot, garnished with fresh parsley if desired.

Nutritional Information (per serving):

- Calories: 275

- Protein: 15g

- Total Fats: 4g

- Fiber: 12g

- Carbohydrates: 46g

Points: 3 Points

Tomato Basil Soup

Time to Prepare: 10 minutes
Cooking Time: 25 minutes
Number of Servings: 4

Ingredients:

- 1 tablespoon olive oil

- 1 onion, diced

- 2 cloves garlic, minced

- 3 cups canned diced tomatoes

- 1 cup of vegetable broth

- 1 teaspoon of dried basil

- 1/2 teaspoon of dried oregano

- Salt and pepper to taste

- 1/4 cup of fresh basil leaves, chopped

- 2 tablespoons grated Parmesan cheese (optional)

Instructions List:

1. In a large pot, heat olive oil over medium heat. Add diced onion and cook until translucent, about 5 minutes.

2. Add minced garlic and cook for another minute.

3. Stir in canned diced tomatoes, vegetable broth, dried basil, dried oregano, salt, and pepper. Bring to a boil.

4. Reduce heat to low and simmer for about 15-20 minutes.

5. Using an immersion blender or regular blender, puree the soup until smooth.

6. Stir in fresh basil leaves and adjust seasoning if needed.

7. Serve hot, garnished with grated Parmesan cheese if desired.

Nutritional Information (per serving):

- Calories: 90

- Protein: 3g

- Total Fats: 4g

- Fiber: 3g

- Carbohydrates: 12g

Points: 2 Points

Moroccan Chickpea Stew

Time to Prepare: 15 minutes
Cooking Time: 30 minutes
Number of Servings: 4

Ingredients:

- 1 tablespoon olive oil

- 1 onion, diced

- 2 cloves garlic, minced

- 1 teaspoon of ground cumin

- 1 teaspoon of ground coriander

- 1/2 teaspoon of ground cinnamon

- 1/4 teaspoon of ground turmeric

- 1/4 teaspoon of cayenne pepper (optional)

- 2 cans (15 ounces each) chickpeas, drained and rinsed

- 1 can (14.5 ounces) diced tomatoes

- 2 cups of vegetable broth

- 2 cups of chopped spinach or kale

- Salt and pepper to taste

- Fresh cilantro, for garnish (optional)

Instructions List:

1. Heat olive oil in a large pot over medium heat. Add diced onion and cook until softened, about 5 minutes.

2. Add minced garlic, ground cumin, ground coriander, ground cinnamon, ground turmeric, and cayenne pepper (if using). Cook for 1 minute until fragrant.

3. Stir in chickpeas, diced tomatoes, and vegetable broth. Bring to a simmer and cook for 20 minutes.

4. Add chopped spinach or kale to the pot and cook until wilted, about 5 minutes.

5. Season with salt and pepper to taste.

6. Serve hot, garnished with fresh cilantro if desired.

Nutritional Information (per serving):

- Calories: 285

- Protein: 10g

- Total Fats: 6g

- Fiber: 11g

- Carbohydrates: 47g

Points: 5 Points

Creamy Broccoli Cheddar Soup

Time to Prepare: 15 minutes
Cooking Time: 25 minutes
Number of Servings: 4

Ingredients:

- 1 tablespoon olive oil

- 1 onion, chopped

- 2 cloves garlic, minced

- 4 cups chopped broccoli florets
- 2 cups of vegetable broth
- 1 cup of unsweetened almond milk (or any milk of choice)
- 1/2 cup of shredded sharp cheddar cheese
- Salt and pepper to taste

Instructions List:

1. Heat olive oil in a large pot over medium heat. Add chopped onion and cook until softened, about 5 minutes.

2. Add minced garlic and cook for another minute until fragrant.

3. Add chopped broccoli florets and vegetable broth to the pot. Bring to a boil, then reduce heat to simmer. Cook for 10-15 minutes until broccoli is tender.

4. Use an immersion blender to blend the soup until smooth. Alternatively, transfer the soup to a blender and blend until smooth, then return it to the pot.

5. Stir in unsweetened almond milk and shredded cheddar cheese until cheese is melted and soup is creamy.

6. Season with salt and pepper to taste.

7. Serve hot.

Nutritional Information (per serving):

- Calories: 165
- Protein: 7g
- Total Fats: 10g
- Fiber: 3g
- Carbohydrates: 14g

Points: 4 Points

Spicy Black Bean Chili

Time to Prepare: 15 minutes
Cooking Time: 30 minutes
Number of Servings: 6

Ingredients:

- 1 tablespoon olive oil
- 1 onion, diced
- 3 cloves garlic, minced
- 2 bell peppers, diced
- 2 teaspoons of ground cumin
- 1 teaspoon of chili powder

- 1/2 teaspoon of smoked paprika

- 1/4 teaspoon of cayenne pepper (adjust to taste)

- 2 (15-ounce) cans black beans, drained and rinsed

- 1 (14.5-ounce) can diced tomatoes

- 1 cup of vegetable broth

- Salt and pepper to taste

- Optional toppings: diced avocado, chopped cilantro, lime wedges, shredded cheese, Greek yogurt

Instructions List:

1. Heat olive oil in a large pot over medium heat. Add diced onion and cook until softened, about 5 minutes.

2. Add minced garlic and diced bell peppers to the pot. Cook for another 3-4 minutes until the peppers are slightly softened.

3. Stir in ground cumin, chili powder, smoked paprika, and cayenne pepper. Cook for 1 minute until fragrant.

4. Add drained black beans, diced tomatoes, and vegetable broth to the pot. Stir to combine.

5. Bring the chili to a simmer, then reduce heat to low. Cover and cook for 20 minutes, stirring occasionally.

6. Season with salt and pepper to taste.

7. Serve hot with optional toppings if desired.

Nutritional Information (per serving):

- Calories: 210

- Protein: 9g

- Total Fats: 4g

- Fiber: 10g

- Carbohydrates: 34g

Points: 3 Points

Chapter 10: Desserts

Chocolate Avocado Mousse

Time to Prepare: 10 minutes
Cooking Time: 0 minutes
Number of Servings: 4

Ingredients:

- 2 ripe avocados
- 1/4 cup of unsweetened cocoa powder
- 1/4 cup of maple syrup or honey
- 1 teaspoon of vanilla extract
- Pinch of salt
- Optional toppings: shaved chocolate, berries, whipped cream

Instructions List:

1. Cut the avocados in half and remove the pits. Scoop the flesh into a blender or food processor.
2. Add cocoa powder, maple syrup or honey, vanilla extract, and a pinch of salt to the blender.
3. Blend until smooth and creamy, scraping down the sides as needed to ensure everything is well mixed.
4. Taste the mousse and adjust sweetness if needed by adding more maple syrup or honey.
5. Transfer the mousse to serving bowls or glasses.
6. Chill in the refrigerator for at least 30 minutes before serving.
7. Serve topped with shaved chocolate, berries, or whipped cream if desired.

Nutritional Information (per serving):

- Calories: 190
- Protein: 2g
- Total Fats: 12g
- Fiber: 7g
- Carbohydrates: 22g

Points: 3 Points

Berry Crumble

Time to Prepare: 15 minutes
Cooking Time: 30 minutes
Number of Servings: 6

Ingredients:

- 4 cups mixed berries (such as strawberries, blueberries, raspberries)

- 2 tablespoons granulated sugar

- 1 tablespoon lemon juice

- 1/2 cup of all-purpose flour

- 1/2 cup of rolled oats

- 1/4 cup of brown sugar

- 1/4 cup of unsalted butter, melted

- 1/2 teaspoon of ground cinnamon

- Pinch of salt

Instructions List:

1. Preheat your oven to 350°F (175°C). Grease a baking dish with butter or cooking spray.

2. In a large bowl, toss the mixed berries with granulated sugar and lemon juice. Spread the berries evenly in the prepared baking dish.

3. In the same bowl, combine the flour, rolled oats, brown sugar, melted butter, cinnamon, and salt. Mix until crumbly.

4. Sprinkle the crumble mixture over the berries in the baking dish.

5. Bake in the preheated oven for 25-30 minutes, or until the crumble topping is golden brown and the berries are bubbling.

6. Remove from the oven and let it cool for a few minutes before serving.

7. Serve warm, optionally with a scoop of vanilla ice cream or a dollop of whipped cream.

Nutritional Information (per serving):

- Calories: 210

- Protein: 3g

- Total Fats: 8g

- Fiber: 5g

- Carbohydrates: 34g

Points: 4 Points

Apple Cinnamon Oat Bars

Time to Prepare: 15 minutes
Cooking Time: 40 minutes
Number of Servings: 12

Ingredients:

- 2 cups of old-fashioned oats

- 1 cup of whole wheat flour

- 1/2 cup of brown sugar

- 1 teaspoon of ground cinnamon

- 1/2 teaspoon of baking powder

- 1/4 teaspoon of salt

- 1/2 cup of unsweetened applesauce

- 1/4 cup of honey

- 1/4 cup of unsalted butter, melted

- 2 medium apples, peeled and diced

Instructions List:

1. Preheat your oven to 350°F (175°C). Grease a 9x13-inch baking dish.

2. In a large bowl, combine the oats, whole wheat flour, brown sugar, cinnamon, baking powder, and salt.

3. In another bowl, mix together the applesauce, honey, and melted butter.

4. Add the wet ingredients to the dry ingredients and stir until well mixed.

5. Fold in the diced apples until evenly distributed throughout the mixture.

6. Press the mixture into the prepared baking dish, spreading it out evenly.

7. Bake in the preheated oven for 35-40 minutes, or until golden brown and set.

8. Remove from the oven and allow to cool completely before cutting into bars.

Nutritional Information (per serving):

- Calories: 180

- Protein: 3g

- Total Fats: 4g

- Fiber: 3g

- Carbohydrates: 34g

Points: 3 Points

Greek Yogurt Popsicles

Time to Prepare: 10 minutes
Freezing Time: 4 hours
Number of Servings: 6

Ingredients:

- 2 cups of plain Greek yogurt

- 1/4 cup of honey or maple syrup

- 1 teaspoon of vanilla extract

- 1 cup of mixed berries (such as strawberries, blueberries, raspberries)

Instructions List:

1. In a mixing bowl, combine the Greek yogurt, honey or maple syrup, and vanilla extract. Stir until well mixed.

2. Divide the mixture evenly among popsicle molds, filling each about 3/4 full.

3. Add the mixed berries to each popsicle mold, using a spoon to press them down into the yogurt mixture.

4. Insert popsicle sticks into the molds.

5. Place the molds in the freezer and freeze for at least 4 hours, or until the popsicles are solid.

6. Once frozen, remove the popsicles from the molds by running them under warm water for a few seconds.

7. Serve immediately or store in the freezer in an airtight container.

Nutritional Information (per serving):

- Calories: 90

- Protein: 6g

- Total Fats: 0g

- Fiber: 1g

- Carbohydrates: 16g

Points: 2 Points

Lemon Ricotta Pancakes

Time to Prepare: 10 minutes
Cooking Time: 15 minutes
Number of Servings: 4

Ingredients:

- 1 cup of all-purpose flour

- 2 tablespoons granulated sugar

- 1 teaspoon of baking powder

- 1/2 teaspoon of baking soda

- 1/4 teaspoon of salt

- 1 cup of part-skim ricotta cheese

- 3/4 cup milk

- 2 large eggs

- 1 tablespoon lemon zest

- 2 tablespoons fresh lemon juice

- Cooking spray or butter, for greasing

Instructions List:

1. In a large bowl, whisk together the flour, sugar, baking powder, baking soda, and salt.

2. In another bowl, combine the ricotta cheese, milk, eggs, lemon zest, and lemon juice. Whisk until smooth.

3. Pour the wet ingredients into the dry ingredients and stir until just mixed. Do not overmix; the batter may be slightly lumpy.

4. Heat a non-stick skillet or griddle over medium heat. Lightly grease the surface with cooking spray or butter.

5. Pour 1/4 cup of batter onto the skillet for each pancake. Cook until bubbles form on the surface and the edges look set, about 2-3 minutes.

6. Flip the pancakes and cook for an additional 1-2 minutes, until golden brown and cooked through.

7. Repeat with the remaining batter, greasing the skillet as needed between batches.

8. Serve the pancakes warm with your favorite toppings, such as fresh berries, maple syrup, or yogurt.

Nutritional Information (per serving):

- Calories: 276

- Protein: 13g

- Total Fats: 8g

- Fiber: 1g

- Carbohydrates: 38g

Points: 5 Points

Pumpkin Spice Energy Bites

Time to Prepare: 10 minutes
Cooking Time: 0 MINUTES
Number of Servings: 12

Ingredients:

- 1 cup of rolled oats

- 1/2 cup of pumpkin puree

- 1/4 cup of almond butter

- 1/4 cup of honey or maple syrup

- 1 teaspoon of vanilla extract

- 1 teaspoon of pumpkin pie spice

- Pinch of salt

- Optional: 1/4 cup of mini chocolate chips or chopped nuts for extra flavor and texture

Instructions List:

1. In a large mixing bowl, combine rolled oats, pumpkin puree, almond butter, honey or maple syrup, vanilla extract, pumpkin pie spice, and a pinch of salt. Stir until well mixed.

2. If desired, fold in mini chocolate chips or chopped nuts.

3. Using your hands, roll the mixture into 12 evenly-sized balls.

4. Place the energy bites on a baking sheet lined with parchment paper and refrigerate for at least 30 minutes to firm up.

5. Once firm, transfer the energy bites to an airtight container and store them in the refrigerator for up to one week.

Nutritional Information (per serving):

- Calories: 88

- Protein: 2g

- Total Fats: 4g

- Fiber: 2g

- Carbohydrates: 12g

Points: 3 Points

Almond Flour Chocolate Chip Cookies

Time to Prepare: 15 minutes
Cooking Time: 10 minutes
Number of Servings: 12 cookies

Ingredients:

- 1 1/2 cups of almond flour

- 1/4 teaspoon of baking soda

- 1/4 teaspoon of salt

- 1/4 cup of melted coconut oil

- 1/4 cup of honey or maple syrup

- 1 teaspoon of vanilla extract

- 1/3 cup dark chocolate chips

Instructions List:

1. Preheat the oven to 350°F (175°C) and line a baking sheet with parchment paper.

2. In a large mixing bowl, whisk together almond flour, baking soda, and salt.

3. Add melted coconut oil, honey or maple syrup, and vanilla extract to the dry ingredients. Stir until well mixed.

4. Fold in the dark chocolate chips.

5. Scoop about 1 tablespoon of dough and roll it into a ball. Place it on the prepared baking sheet. Repeat with the remaining dough, spacing the cookies about 2 inches apart.

6. Flatten each cookie slightly with the palm of your hand.

7. Bake for 10-12 minutes or until the edges are golden brown.

8. Remove from the oven and let the cookies cool on the baking sheet for 5 minutes before transferring them to a wire rack to cool completely.

Nutritional Information (per serving):

- Calories: 148

- Protein: 3g

- Total Fats: 11g

- Fiber: 1g

- Carbohydrates: 11g

Points: 4 Points

Mixed Berry Salad

Time to Prepare: 10 minutes
Cooking Time: 0 minutes
Number of Servings: 4 servings

Ingredients:

- 4 cups of mixed berries (such as strawberries, blueberries, raspberries, blackberries)

- 2 tablespoons fresh lemon juice

- 1 tablespoon honey (optional)

- Fresh mint leaves for garnish (optional)

Instructions List:

1. Rinse the mixed berries under cold water and pat them dry with a paper towel. Slice any large berries into bite-sized pieces if necessary.

2. In a large mixing bowl, gently toss the berries with fresh lemon juice until they are evenly coated.

3. If desired, drizzle the honey over the berries and toss again to combine.

4. Transfer the mixed berry salad to a serving bowl or divide it among individual serving plates.

5. Garnish with fresh mint leaves, if using.

6. Serve immediately or refrigerate until ready to serve.

Nutritional Information (per serving):

- Calories: 70

- Protein: 1g

- Total Fats: 0g

- Fiber: 5g

- Carbohydrates: 18g

Points: 0 Points

Baked Apples with Cinnamon

Time to Prepare: 10 minutes
Cooking Time: 25 minutes
Number of Servings: 4 servings

Ingredients:

- 4 medium-sized apples

- 1 teaspoon of ground cinnamon

- 1/4 teaspoon of ground nutmeg (optional)

- 1 tablespoon granulated sweetener (such as erythritol or stevia) (optional)

- 1/4 cup of water

Instructions List:

1. Preheat your oven to 375°F (190°C).

2. Wash the apples thoroughly and remove the cores using an apple corer or a knife, leaving the bottoms intact.

3. In a small bowl, mix together the ground cinnamon, ground nutmeg (if using), and granulated sweetener (if using).

4. Place the cored apples in a baking dish. Sprinkle the cinnamon mixture evenly over each apple.

5. Pour the water into the bottom of the baking dish.

6. Cover the baking dish with aluminum foil and bake in the preheated oven for about 20-25 minutes, or until the apples are tender.

7. Once baked, remove the foil and let the apples cool slightly before serving.

Nutritional Information (per serving):

- Calories: 60

- Protein: 0g

- Total Fats: 0g

- Fiber: 5g

- Carbohydrates: 16g

Points: 0 Points

Watermelon Granita

Time to Prepare: 10 minutes
Cooking Time: 4 hours freezing time
Number of Servings: 4 servings

Ingredients:

- 4 cups of cubed seedless watermelon

- 2 tablespoons fresh lime juice

- 2 tablespoons honey or agave syrup (optional)
- Fresh mint leaves, for garnish (optional)

Instructions List:

1. Place the cubed watermelon in a blender or food processor.
2. Add the fresh lime juice and honey or agave syrup (if using).
3. Blend until smooth.
4. Pour the mixture into a shallow baking dish or a large freezer-safe container.
5. Place the dish in the freezer and let it freeze for about 1 hour.
6. After 1 hour, remove the dish from the freezer and use a fork to scrape the mixture, breaking up any ice crystals that have formed.
7. Return the dish to the freezer and repeat the scraping process every 30 minutes for about 3 hours, or until the mixture is completely frozen and has a slushy texture.
8. Once frozen, use a fork to scrape the granita into fluffy ice crystals.
9. Serve immediately in chilled glasses, garnished with fresh mint leaves if desired.

Nutritional Information (per serving):

- Calories: 50
- Protein: 1g
- Total Fats: 0g
- Fiber: 1g
- Carbohydrates: 13g

Points: 0 Points

MEASUREMENT CONVERSION TABLE

Measurement	Imperial (US)	Metric
Volume		
1 teaspoon	1 tsp	5 milliliters
1 tablespoon	1 tbsp	15 milliliters
1 fluid ounce	1 fl oz	30 milliliters
1 cup	1 cup	240 milliliters
1 pint	1 pt	473 milliliters
1 quart	1 qt	0.95 liters
1 gallon	1 gal	3.8 liters
Weight		
1 ounce	1 oz	28 grams
1 pound	1 lb	454 grams
Temperature		
32°F	32°F	0°C
212°F	212°F	100°C
Other		
1 stick of butter	1 stick	113 grams

CONCLUSION

Congratulations on starting your Freestyle journey! I've compiled this collection of recipes to provide you with a wide range of tasty and healthy choices that perfectly align with your way of living. We have a diverse range of dishes available, including breakfast scrambles, comforting soups, and sweet treats. Keep in mind that Freestyle places a strong emphasis on achieving balance and flexibility. Feel free to try different variations of these recipes to suit your taste. As you continue this book, consider your Points budget and prioritize mindful eating. Enjoy each mouthful and take pride in your accomplishments beyond the numbers on the scale. By committing yourself and drawing inspiration from these recipes, you'll make significant progress towards your weight loss objectives and cultivate a positive connection with food.

RECIPE INDEX

Moroccan Chickpea Stew 102

Moroccan Spiced Chicken Tagine 31

Oatmeal Raisin Cookies 26

Orange-Glazed Turkey Cutlets 38

Pesto Stuffed Chicken Breast 39

Pork Tenderloin with Apple Chutney 57

Portobello Mushroom Burger 85

Pumpkin Spice Energy Bites 110

Pumpkin Spice Muffins 22

Quinoa Breakfast Bowl 8

Quinoa Flatbread 23

Quinoa-Stuffed Bell Peppers 48

Ratatouille 86

Red Lentil Soup 53

Roasted Vegetable Quinoa Bowl 78

Rosemary Olive Oil Focaccia 21

Sesame Ginger Glazed Mahi Mahi 75

Shrimp and Zucchini Noodles 71

Shrimp Scampi Zoodles 67

Slow Cooker Cider-Braised Pulled Chicken Sandwiches 37

Smoked Salmon and Avocado Toast 76

Southern-Style Oven-Fried Chicken 35

Spicy Black Bean Chili 104

Spicy Thai Beef Salad 65

Spinach and Ricotta Stuffed Shells 87

Stuffed Bell Peppers with Quinoa and Black Beans 79

Sweet Potato and Black Bean Enchiladas 88

Teriyaki Turkey Burgers 33

Thai Basil Chicken Stir-Fry 41

Thai Coconut Curry Soup 93

Tofu Scramble 6

Tomato Basil Soup 101

Tuna Salad Lettuce Wraps 69

Turkey and Black Bean Chili 59

Tuscan Chicken Skillet 34

Vegetable Lentil Soup 96

Veggie-Packed Breakfast Burrito 3

Watermelon Granita 113

White Bean and Kale Soup 94

Whole Wheat Banana Bread 20

Wild Rice Pilaf 50

Zucchini Fritters with Tzatziki 11

Zucchini Noodles with Pesto 84

Made in the USA
Coppell, TX
15 October 2024

38723658R00070